PRINCIPLES OF LANGUAGE TESTING

Applied Language Studies
Edited by David Crystal and Keith Johnson

This new series aims to deal with key topics within the main branches of applied language studies — initially in the fields of foreign language teaching and learning, child language acquisition and clinical or remedial language studies. The series will provide students with a research perspective in a particular topic, at the same time containing an original slant which will make each volume a genuine contribution to the development of ideas in the subject.

Series List

PRINCIPLES OF
LANGUAGE TESTING

Alan Davies

Basil Blackwell

First published 1990

Basil Blackwell Ltd
108 Cowley Road, Oxford, OX4 1JF, UK

Basil Blackwell, Inc.
3 Cambridge Center
Cambridge, Massachusetts 02142, USA

British Library Cataloguing in Publication Data

A CIP catalogue record for this book is available from the British Library.

Library of Congress Cataloguing in Publication Data

Davies, Alan, Ph. D.
    Principles of language testing / Alan Davies.
        p.   cm. — (Applied language studies)
    Includes bibliographical references.
    ISBN 0−631−17342−0   ISBN 0−631−17343−9 (pbk.)
    1. Language and languages — Ability testing. I. Title.
II. Series: Applied language studies (Basil Blackwell Publisher)
P53.4.D37   1990
418′.0076 — dc20   90−1441
                                                                    CIP

Typeset in 10 on 12 pt Ehrhardt
by Setrite Typesetters Ltd, Hong Kong
Printed in Great Britain by T.J. Press Ltd, Padstow, Cornwall

Contents

Preface

The purpose of this book is to attempt a coherent view of language testing, placing it firmly within the field of applied linguistics. Many of the ideas have appeared in earlier publications and these are all acknowledged in the list of references. For many years I avoided writing a book on language testing, partly because I felt it had all been said before by others, and partly because I was perhaps over-influenced by the general view of the marginality of language testing. As I try to show in the following chapters, that view cannot now seriously be supported. Having originally become involved by accident in language testing and tried for years to escape into a more respectable field, I have come to realize that there is no need after all to escape, because what was once thought to be marginal has now become part of the main stream. Perhaps there is a moral there for other aspects of life: not to think oneself too odd. I try to explain how language testing has come to be appreciated both for its techniques and, perhaps more important, for the operationalizing it can offer in applied linguistics. That change has of course come about only because there has continued to be serious and important work in language testing, and I like to think that through my work over the years I have helped in a small way to bring it about.

I came into the subject in the early 1960s. After spending some years as a teacher of English as a mother tongue in UK secondary schools and then of English as a second language in Kenya, I found myself in Birmingham working on an MA on négritude in African writing in English. After some months' research pursuing what seemed to me more and more a snark-like idea, especially among Anglophone writers, I was offered a paid research post in the Department of Education in Birmingham University. I was to work on the development of an English language proficiency test for overseas students coming to study in British universities and other institutions of higher education. The project was funded by the British Council who were anxious at that time to make their selection of candidates for scholarships and fellowships more objective. In due course I produced the English Proficiency Test Battery which was used by the British Council world-wide between 1965 and 1980. Four versions of the test were eventually produced, version 3 in collaboration with Alan Moller and version 4 with Charles Alderson. I want here to record my thanks to those two colleagues who at the time were research students of mine. And I want also to express my gratitude to four colleagues from the Birmingham period; Arthur King of the British Council who saw the need for this work, George Perren also of the British Council who made it all happen, Edwin Peel of Birmingham University who supervised my own research for the work on proficiency testing, and Vera Adamson for her supportiveness.

After Birmingham I went on to Edinburgh. But that is another story.

Acknowledgements

I want to thank all those who have helped me see the use and the interest of language testing, and I dedicate the book to Anne, Ben, Sara, Megan and Hester who have survived it all with me.

Alan Davies
Edinburgh

1 Introduction

Language testing is central to language teaching. It provides goals for language teaching, and it monitors, for both teachers and learners, success in reaching those goals. Its influence on teaching (the notorious 'backwash' or 'washback' effect) is strong – and is usually felt to be wholly negative. It provides a methodology for experiment and investigation in both language teaching and language learning/acquisition. So potent an influence, so salient a presence, deserves much closer attention and study than it typically receives. Compared with writings about language teaching, whether methodology, syllabus, materials or theory, those about language testing are very small beer indeed. No doubt this is partly because of suspicion of the quantitative methods of test analysis and the strong conviction that humane, cultural knowledge does not reduce to mere numbers.

It is normal for teaching to be directed towards assessment, sometimes labelled *examination*. Such 'washback' is so widely prevalent that it makes sense to accept it, to stop regarding is as negative, and then make it as good as it can be in order to improve its influence to the maximum. What cannot (or is unlikely to) happen is that the assessment will have no effect. And yet, curiously, such an attitude seems very common. Observe:

1 the lack of thought given to the construction of most language examinations where the chief check is on the scoring rather than on the preparation;
2 the ignoring of how serious an influence on teaching the examination has. Here indeed is an interesting and relevant distinction between the idea of the test and of the examination. It is accepted, generally, that tests are influential and require careful planning and administration. Such care is less often given to examinations.

We shall argue that examinations are special kinds of test: our discussion will generally ignore differences. We shall consider practical and theoretical aspects of language tests, as well as their research role and their contribution to the development of speculative accounts and theoretical statements about language and language learning.

Our view is that language testing is rightly central to language teaching. As such it belongs most appropriately within the discipline of Applied Linguistics. The purpose of this book is to celebrate that centrality and to examine the interrelationship of language testing, language teaching and applied linguistics, raising the question of just how far testing is servant and how far master.

Discussions of language testing are typically instrumental and mechanistic, concerning the how and the what (Oller 1979, Henning 1987). What is needed, and what we attempt to offer, is a more humanistic account of the scope and role of language testing. We shall be concerned with questions such as: what is testing for? the *why* of testing as opposed to the *what* and the *how*. We will argue strongly for the leadership role of language testing and for the positive influence of washback. We will also emphasize the contribution of language testing to applied linguistics of which, in our view, it is now firmly part. We shall further discuss the extent to which applied linguistics has influenced developments in language testing. It is our view, and we shall explain this more fully later, that language testing has become the major cutting edge of applied linguistics and that an applied linguistics without language testing is now inconceivable.

The book does not attempt to cover the whole field of language testing and so does not set out to be an introductory textbook. Other books have that role (Oller 1979, Henning 1987, Hughes 1989, Bachman 1990), but our purpose is to suggest the range and scope of language testing within applied linguistics, and thereby, it is hoped, to support the argument for its central role. What language testing offers applied linguistics is:

1   an operationalizing of its theoretical constructs;
2   a means of establishing goals and standards for teaching courses and syllabuses;
3   a methodology for carrying out empirical research in applied linguistics, whether that research is language testing (*tout court*) research; investigations in language acquisition, judgements, intelligibility studies, comprehension and use; or comparative experiments in language teaching methodologies and materials.

What language testing does is to compel attention to the meaning of ideas in linguistics and applied linguistics. Until they are put into operation, described and explained, ideas can remain ambiguous and fugitive. A test forces choice, removes ambiguity and reveals what has been elusive: thus a test is the most explicit form of description, on the basis of which the tester comes clean about his/her ideas. This holds good for all testing but is especially so for language tests since the nature of language is to be both infinite and unlistable. As such, it is unlike both creative skills (such as music) and content subjects (such as history) and is therefore a special case.

This special case of language and language learning has three bases: the knowledge–control relationship; the sampling question; and the problem of defining an external criterion other than the test itself. Language ability seems to depend on both knowledge and control, a relationship that cannot be finally teased apart. The balance between knowing the language and knowing about the language remains problematic.

The sampling problem of language testing affects all language interventions, the linguist's, the teacher's and the tester's. Of necessity they all use samples, since in no way can the *whole* of a living language ever be described, taught or tested, and all the samples are, paradoxically, both totally inadequate and totally adequate at the same time. Let me explain for the tester's samples — a similar argument could be adduced for the linguist's sample and the teacher's. A tester's samples are inadequate because no sample can represent the variability and the infinite nature of language; at the same time they are wholly adequate because of the generative nature of language which acts as its own creative source.

The demands on language testing are therefore severe. 'This test', the tester claims, 'represents, stands for, *is* the language' (the claim that the linguist makes for his/her grammar and the teacher for his/her textbook/ materials/syllabus). For that reason, in spite of the extreme view we have just expressed — that any sample will do — it must be the case that serious language testing is very sample conscious. Apart from any other consideration, while the samples encapsulated in the linguist's grammar and the teacher's textbook have some body and occupy a reading/studying/teaching and learning space time of many hours, the test is typically quite short. Indeed a language proficiency test of more than 3 hours is often thought to be excessively long. And yet how much of the language (and this a dilemma especially for the overall proficiency test) can be contained within 3 hours?

Vagueness also comes from the very imprecision of a language-related criterion. The issue here is that the buttressing validity of an external criterion is often neither definable nor, when found, reliable. Take, for example, two well-known examples: the language achievement test given at the end of a period of secondary school language instruction, and a language proficiency test used to determine adequacy for academic study in that language medium. What external criterion can be appealed to in these two situations? In the first is it teachers' judgements, is it success in higher education, is it appropriate behaviour in a real-world encounter which requires language use? In the second is it success in the student's own studies at the end of the academic course (degree, diploma, PhD), or is it general well-being and contentment during the course of study? None of these is definable except in very imprecise ways. The success in academic studies may appear to be definable, unlike, say, the 'general well-being and contentment' which is inaccessible to objective view, but it is by no means always clear what constitutes success; or, rather, what constitutes failure. In Davies (1984b) it emerged that 'failure' (and therefore 'success') could be demonstrated only at the end of a very long time: for example, does a PhD student who continues registration for 10 years count as a failure each year? Furthermore, even such success is not clearly attributable to language in that it must be related to so many other variables (general and special ability, hard work and application; health, motivation, luck and so on).

What is sometimes said, of course, is that this is trivial argumentation which can be answered, like Alexander cutting the Gordian knot or like Dr Johnson kicking the stone to refute Bishop Berkeley. That is to say that we know success, fluency and proficiency when we observe them. Alas! that no-nonsense approach will not do, because observers do not necessarily agree with one another, and we are back once more at our attempts to control what we can control, that is, the test: back on our circular route of the test as best criterion.

The inadequacy of the criterion, its unreliability and frequent non-validity, underlies the enduring argument − which we discuss later − about direct and indirect tests. If it is indeed the case, as we have argued, that there is no criterion out there and that it is after all the responsibility of the test itself to establish, in a wholly circular manner, its own criterion, then one extrapolation from that logic is to suggest that a direct test (for example, a performance oral test) has no special value over an indirect test (for example, a dictation test or even a grammar test) since there is no reliable performance which can be trusted as the criterion. So the indirect test can act as its own criterion just as effectively as the direct test can. Fortunately for our claims for language testing, and our sanity, we cannot be so categorical. Neither the external criterion nor the direct test is so hopeless or vacuous that we should abandon them so cavalierly. As we shall see.

We shall need to take account of the three areas on which language testing draws − *language, measurement* and *language ability* − and in so doing look ahead to related parts of the book.

Language

Language may be viewed from differing points of view: from the linguistic, including the psycholinguistic and the sociolinguistic, from the applied linguistic, including the language teaching and learning, and from that of the lay person. *The linguistic view* regards language as made up of systems (for example, the intonation system, the tense system) which interlock and relate both to one another and to non-language domains. Systems are structurally constituted and structurally related. The major linguistic systems are those of phonology, grammar and semantics with phonetics and discourse marking the extremes where systems become less clearly systematic.

The psycholinguistic view regards language as cognitive, associated with development, with learning and thinking and above all with production processes. The definition of ability in language is marginally psycholinguistic since all tests are concerned with performance in relation to some notional underlying competence and, therefore, with the linking processes.

The sociolinguistic view regards language as inherently variable across time and space but systematically so. Thus the twin purposes of sociolinguistic endeavour are (1) to incorporate social contexts and processes in linguistic theory and descriptions such that linguistic rules will specify the influence of social conditioning on the output of the rules, and (2) to map the (systematic) relationship between language and society, that is to regard language utterances as social facts. To some extent this second aspect of sociolinguistics is as much the concern (perhaps more the concern) of sociology as of linguistics, nevertheless it is by no means clear at what point the study of linguistic variation ends and that of social facts begins. For example gender-related speech may be regarded from both viewpoints as one aspect of systematic variation in terms of social variable, and as a form of social fact conveying information about male and female roles in society. Similarly, bilingual switching may be regarded from the society point of view as languages in contact or language loss or maintenance, or from that of a process similar to that of creolization and therefore as the sociolinguistic influence of social process on language change. However, in terms of the concerns of language testing, it is the first point of view, that of the incorporation of variation within linguistics, that is of interest and relevance.

Just as linguistics has tried to come to terms with language variation at the centre (it always did at the periphery in the shape of dialectology) by extending linguistic descriptions into pragmatics and discourse and raising the claims of variable or 'squishy' rules (Ross 1979) and so on, so must language testing become more tolerant and thereby more rich. But the difficulty caused to linguistic flexibility by practical idealization is not as great as the difficulty for measurement because of the requirement of norms. What is perhaps more immediately hopeful is not the incorporation of sociolinguistic variation into testing protocols but the accessibility to test construction of developing procedures and recognized methods in the study of Second-Language Acquisition, the Interlanguage continuum, which makes no claims for varieties other than ontogenetic ones.

Measurement

Taking account, as we shall, of uncertainty within confidence limits, accuracy in measurement is based on estimates of *reliability* and *validity*. Reliability is measured directly in various ways which can be generalized to a comparison between one set of items and a comparable set in order to estimate consistency of measure. Reliability is also estimated by the amount of indeterminacy in a test score in terms of the Standard Error of Measurement, on the logical assumption that the larger the spread of scores around a mean the more likely that they are replicable: the negative aspect of this would be for everyone to achieve the same score, a result which in terms of reliability carries no information.

Item analysis is part reliability, part validity, the assumption being that items with modestly high discrimination are likely also to be replicable, and that that very discrimination is itself an augur of a satisfactory test construct, that is, of the items belonging together. The purpose of item analysis is to determine test homogeneity: the more similar to one another (without being identical) test items are, the more likely it is that they are measuring in the same area and therefore that they are doing something useful (validity) and doing it consistently (reliability). Both aspects give credence to the (often forgotten) need to sum across items in order to produce test scores. The more homogeneous the items, the more sensible it is to add them − just as in a tape measure the assumption is that the second centimetre or inch can be added to the first and so on, that is, that they are additive. Other methods of item analysis (for example item response theory) will be mentioned later.

While reliability is concerned with ensuring that a test is a measure (i.e. that whatever it is that it measures it does so accurately), validity has to do with that 'whatever it is' and attempts to provide a theoretical framework which gives reassurance to the test. It is not surprising that there are several kinds of validity. They are listed below, but it should be noted that they are all concerned with the relation between the test instrument and the domain to be measured. As will be evident, the definition of domain can be quite close, as in face validity, or quite distant, as in construct validity (see chapter 3).

Test measurement is also a practical matter. It is important to remember (and to recall) that testing is possible only if it is practicable. A good test (highly valid and reliable) may in practice be unusable because in the situation for which it is intended it would take up too much time, too much skilled manpower, or it might require expensive or elaborate media systems or scoring arrangements, and so on. How then (it might be asked) does one know that it is both valid and reliable? That is a very fair question, and on one interpretation of 'valid' it would have to be admitted, that if it is not practical it must lack validity because it is unusable on its target population. And yet it is possible to establish reliability and validity on a laboratory sample and then, as a result of that application, to recognize the impracticality under less favourable conditions.

Language Ability

Language ability must be seen in terms of test use and test purpose. We may distinguish at least 5 uses: achievement, proficiency, aptitude, diagnosis, and pre-achievement. Two main test purposes may be distinguished, norm-referenced and criterion-referenced. These are discussed more fully in chapter 2 but we will refer briefly to them here.

In *achievement (or attainment)* the concern is with measuring what has been learnt of what has been taught or what is in the syllabus, text book, materials, etc. Achievement tests are, in other words, based on a clear and public indication of the instruction that has been given. *Proficiency*, on the other hand, is concerned not with publicly stated instruction but with the relationship between language control and a particular use of language, for example, with whether a testee has adequate language for academic study, for practising as a doctor, for working as a pilot, for driving a car, for being a ski instructor and so on.

Aptitude tests measure language learning ability. In doing so they attempt to incorporate the dynamic (the process) of language learning that achievement and proficiency tests signally fail to do since they are (by their nature) static tests, testing ability and knowledge at one point in time. Aptitude tests on the other hand seek to indicate capacity for growth. *Diagnostic* tests do exist in name, but it is not obvious that they differ seriously from proficiency tests. A 'true' diagnostic test seeks to plot learning to date (in certain specified areas) and sets out, through the student profile arrived at, to characterize what is needed in order to remedy error. *Pre-achievement* is in fact a special case of achievement testing, in which a test design is based not on the instruction that has been given, but on the instruction to come after. Many admissions tests are of this kind since they are content related to the syllabus that will be followed. They operate as screening, level-finding tests and those whose performance is very good will of course be excluded from all following instruction.

Norm-referenced tests are based on the notion of the normal distribution of attributes (such as height) and abilities (such as intelligence, language). It is no doubt the case that the notion may be unreal, or that the tests that do distribute normally do so only because they have been designed to do so, not because they necessarily mirror reality. Norm referencing makes use of rank orders; it places individuals on a scale. Recent discussions of *criterion referencing* (see chapter 2) have seemed to suggest that it is a new development in that it replaces ranks by criteria or goals which are task related: the emphasis is now on discriminating tasks rather than individuals. But as with the analogies, high and long jumps (see p. 19), criterion referencing has always been a particular use of norm referencing in that a level of achievement or proficiency (a 'pass') has often been set, but one which did not necessarily select out a set proportion in a mindless way. Criterion referencing and norm referencing are essentially two sides of the same phenomenon: one side looks at what people can do, the other side at what they need to do.

The chapters that follow are all related to a general theme: the need to accept creatively the compromise between the underlying *uncertainty* of language testing and its need for *explicitness*. The more usual terms used for these concepts are *reliability* and *validity* and we shall use these terms extensively, but for the moment we wish to insist that the compromise is a more general one, hence the use of the terms *uncertainty* and *explicitness*.

Chapter 2 provides definitions for the terms and concepts used in the book and is developed out of the discussion so far in this Introduction. In chapter 3 we move on from definitions to a consideration of the information that language testing can provide. After the defining and the boundary marking, an attempt is made in chapter 4 to begin the locating of language testing in applied linguistics. Our first attempt at this is through the concept of continuum categories. Our view, which is taken up again in chapter 5, is that language testing is, as we have already seen, a compromise between the known and the unknown, represented by *validity* and *reliability* and also by other polarities. We model these continua and suggest a reconciling through validity and reliability.

Chapter 5 concerns the central topic of *uncertainty* and *explicitness*, and here we come on to the chief message of this present enquiry: language testing must not avoid the necessary compromise between the two poles symbolized by the majestic division between *validity* and *reliability*, drawn as the super-ordinate polar tension. Chapter 6 sets out the argument for the central role of language testing in applied linguistics. Here the various arguments which are supplied throughout the book are assembled together to provide strong support for the interaction between *uncertainty* and *explicitness*. At the same time this chapter has the parallel purpose of commenting on current issues in language testing.

Chapters 7, 8 and 9 extend the discussion to the use of language testing in various types of evaluation. In chapter 7, on evaluation methodology for different methods and contents, it is noted that evaluation may concern questions about the learning, the achievement and the learning means. Six types of language testing research are then outlined and those not already dealt with are considered in more detail. These range from research using test data to testing research into other applied linguistic fields. Chapters 8 and 9 use the methodologies set out in chapter 7 to discuss in some detail examples of these various kinds of test evaluation. The claim that language testing, operating as a humane compromise between uncertainty and explicitness, functions centrally in applied linguistic studies is emphasized through these examples.

2 Requirements of Language Tests

The Messages of Language Tests

Language testing, like error analysis, comes from a long and honourable tradition of practical teaching and learning need. In recent years it has found itself taken up as a methodology for the probing and investigation of language ability (and therefore of language itself) much as error analysis was taken up, first by contrastive studies, and later by second-language acquisition research (see chapter 6). The practical tradition of language testing continues, often under the name of language examining: language examinations, that is exercises and tasks of all kinds, which, it is assumed, are at the proper standard, are used throughout education to make judgements about progress and to predict future performance. Such language examinations, as in other subjects taught at school and college, are used for selection, for feedback and, less frequently, for evaluation and research.

Language testing represents a measured concentration on language use and knowledge. Apart from its obvious practical relevance, what makes *language testing* important within applied linguistics is:

1 that unlike other subjects offered to students in education a language has no obvious content. This appears to make it less like, say, mathematics, science and history and more like musical performance and sports. There is a continuing debate about the role of knowledge in language ability and the extent to which such knowledge is necessary for, and can overtly be offered to, learners. Assessing language produces complications regarding what is to be tested (trying to reach agreement on the content, this is the issue of *validity*), and how the testing is to be done (trying to reach agreement on the appropriate testing methods so as to be consistent, this is the issue of *reliability*).

2 that in the remarkable natural acquisition of language by humans, which again distances language from other school subjects − this time making it more like culture and art on the one hand and biological development on the other − language testing has a research role within language study which is denied the testing of, for example, chemistry in studies of chemistry.

Chemists do not need, it appears, to draw on information from school-based tests of chemistry in order to develop ideas about chemistry. This is not to deny that such data can be useful in demonstrating aspects of learners' understanding of chemistry: whether courses are running too fast or too slow, to what extent all humans find they can understand chemistry, and at what ages they do so. Language testing, on the other hand, has a useful research role in itself − into the nature of language as well as into language acquisition − and all this in addition to doing what subject tests typically help explain, the extent of subject learning. The crucial difference between language (or culture) in education and other curriculum areas, like chemistry, is surely *the native speaker*, that we believe there is a native speaker of a language but not a 'native speaker' of chemistry.

In order to discuss the uses of language testing as well as the purposes it attempts to serve, we propose to consider the links between testing in general and language testing in particular. Language testing is based on educational testing which itself derives from measurement theory and practice in psychology and psychometrics. The elicitation methods which are also used in some areas of language testing are more closely related to sociological and anthropological field work than to education. The testing component of a language test necessarily imposes constraints, precisely psychometric constraints; we shall consider to what extent the language component is powerful enough to require a relaxing of the psychometric constraints. What matters is that a language test combines both aspects, that it is about *language* and that it is a *test*. I have suggested that school tests of other subjects do not have to meet this double requirement in the same way. Such a double requirement leads inevitably to a tension between the demands of language and those of testing. The extent to which a language test succeeds is a measure of how far it manages to reconcile those twin requirements.

However, although the special nature of language (as a skill and as part of normal human development) may make it less like straightforward educational subjects, these very qualities make it much closer than those other subjects to the concerns of psychology, with its careful study and assessment of human behaviour. This is particularly true for first-language development where the influence of psychological studies of child development has been very strong. The methodology of psychological measurement has also been influential in charting and assessing child development. This applies not only in first-language studies: it has also influenced second-language studies, both in the closely related research into second-language acquisition through the influence of research into first-language development, and through ideas derived from psychology about learning (of skills, styles, and mastery) as well as about testing concepts and methods.

It is not suprising that language testing should bring together so many interests both practical and theoretical since it provides a focus for the *triple message* that language assessment always provides:

1   a message about skill, to what extent learners have reached adequate proficiency, however that is defined, and the role of language tests in developing more specific and detailed indicators of adequate proficiencies.
2   a message about development, which appears at first sight only to be psycholinguistic since it seems to suggest a progress along a very clear and obvious path towards some kind of obvious adult goal. That obviousness is not true even of native speakers among whom goals differ widely. Second-/ foreign-language learners are less varied in that they are likely to be organized so as to proceed along very clear (standard-language, native-speaker) routes. They are also more varied since for them what matters is the attainment of some specified goal level and all language proficiency contains a large number of possible − and usable − levels of achievement. Attached to this message about development for all language learners is an indication of the identity which the learner chooses (usually unconsciously). Information about development therefore provides an indication − through assessment − as to the psycholinguistic and the sociolinguistic provenance of the learner.
3   a message about knowledge. Language users, both native speakers and non-native speakers, distinguish themselves in terms of their awareness of language. This shows itself both in the range of acceptability judgements they are prepared to make and in the extent of their conscious metalinguistic reflecting upon language, which in turn demonstrates itself in knowledge about language and in areas of ludic creativity. Such a reification of language does seem to discriminate both among native speakers and among non-natives; it does, of course, have some bearing on our first message, that of skill, since there may well be an element of knowledge within skill which determines differential proficiency.

Stages of Test Construction

References used in language testing discussions often refer to psychological work. It is therefore of interest to consider to what extent language tests are a sub-category of psychological tests. Many of the principles and procedures involved in language test construction derive from psychological testing. Indeed, there is a view which says that a language test is a psychological test with a specialist content and that therefore constructors of language tests need to learn about testing rather than about language. (In our judgement this is true only if the test constructor already has a specialist knowledge of language through professional work as a language teacher or linguist.)

Anstey (1966) states that psychological tests can be defined as 'devices for the quantitative assessment of psychological attributes of an individual' and he quotes with approval Anastasi (1961): 'a psychological test is an objective and standardised measure of a sample of behaviour'. Anstey distinguishes between cognitive tests (of ability or knowledge) and tests which are mainly non-cognitive or 'personality' tests. He also points out that the distinction between cognitive and non-cognitive tests is artificial in that the distinction between personality and knowledge is not clear-cut. Some tests have been used for both when administered or scored in different ways. For our purposes the distinction has the value that it enables us to distinguish between, on the one hand, language tests of the achievement, proficiency and diagnostic kinds as being more cognitive and, on the other hand, tests of the aptitude kind as less cognitive. But even that distinction remains debatable.

When he comes to describing the stages of psychological test construction Anstey could well be discussing language tests. He suggests four stages, as follows:

Stage 1.   Plan the content and general layout of the test, decide on the type of test item, the length and time limit for the test in its final form, the instructions to be given and the method for scoring. This is the *planning* stage.

Stage 2.   Devise at least three times as many items as will eventually be needed (more if two parallel versions are likely to be required) and try the rough draft on a small group of interested people in order to obtain introspections on the general impact of the test, and to identify items which are palpably unsatisfactory. This is the *prepilot* stage.

Stage 3.   A try-out, preferably two or more try-outs of successive drafts, on a large sample of the same kind of people on whom the test is to be used, in order to check the test administration and provide material for thorough item analysis and revision of the draft test. This may be called the *pilot* stage.

Stage 4.   Try-out of the test in its final form in order to obtain evidence as to its practical usefulness or validity and to obtain 'norms', that is means of assessing the significance of scores in the test. This is the *final validation* stage.

Stages 2, 3 and 4 are partly procedural — they employ the techniques of item analysis and descriptive statistics — and partly dependent on the success of Stage 1. It is important to be clear as to what Stage 1 involves, since it is at this stage that the professional language knowledge of the test constructor is called upon. Stage 1, Anstey tells us, is when we plan the content and general lay-out of the test and decide on the type of test item. Information on this stage is scarce: the process of item planning and writing is rarely described in any detail. This is a pity because this stage is crucial for language sampling and hence for subsequent test validation.

Language test construction is carried out either by one individual who has been hired to produce a test or by a working party. In either case there is likely to be an agreed blueprint or set of specifications (Anstey's 'content and general layout'). This being so, whether the item writing is done by one person or by a working party is incidental. What matters is the decision embodied in the blueprint as to what the test is to consist of. It is likely that the test designer(s) of a proficiency test will wish to sample both the language system and the use of the language system. Although there is continuing disagreement as to the relative importance of these two areas in summarizing the learner's language proficiency it is likely that a proficiency test will contain elements of both. If the test reflects the psychometric–structuralist view of language test construction (Spolsky 1977), then it may concentrate on the *language system*, while if it reflects more the psycholinguistic–sociolinguistic view it will deal more with the *use of the language system*.

Aims, Concepts, Constraints

What does knowing a language mean? We assume that the fugitive ideal native speaker is the exponent of that knowledge but what that knowledge is remains vague and a matter of approximate guessing. Those professionally involved in language description, the linguist, the language teacher and the language tester all approach the issue of encapsulating the native speaker's knowledge through some form of selection or sampling.

The *linguist* (typically the grammarian) chooses representative native speakers (sometimes as few as one) who can provide information about sentence formation and so on. The evidence available to the linguist and the description he or she provides is bound to be partial and is likely to be most valid as a linguistic description the more abstract it is, that is the further away from the idiolectal details of those informants who were sampled.

The *language teacher* also, and necessarily, samples the language in making it available to the learner. Given the amount of time usually available for learning a second or foreign language in an institutional setting (a maximum of, say, 1000 hours over 5 years as against, say, 25 000 hours for the child acquiring his/her first language up to the age of 5) the teacher can select only what are thought to be key items, critical points and so on. A traditional way of handling the shortage of time is to make the teaching selection as much like the linguist's/grammarian's as possible, in other words to provide an overtly rule-based selection which can be learnt off in the time available and which is both generalizable and potentially deployable. More recent approaches (Morrow 1979) have claimed that knowing the rules thus overtly is unrelated to language proficiency and to the ability to use language. Such approaches provide for an exposure to situational and communicative language use, that is to situated rule-based behaviour, thereby providing both the rule (through example) and the use of the rule.

These approaches are obviously based on a simulation of first-language acquisition; from our point of view what is important is not whether they work but whether or not they can be said to avoid the need for sampling, that is making choices about generalizability. The answer must of course be that they do not. All exposure which is less than the total submersion of the first-language child acquirer must be partial. A common-sense reconciling of the two types of approach would suggest that the traditional one is more likely to cover the language if only a short time is available; the more recent communicative approaches are likely to make their point about language use if a longer time is available. But if a longer time is available, the more traditional approaches too are likely to use the extra time not for inculcating yet more learning about rules, but rather for practice in using the rules. And so the two types of method are likely – if they have enough time available – to come together. *Enough time* is likely to approximate closely to the amount required for first-language acquisition and, since this is never available in institutional settings, we can safely assume that all language teaching involves sampling and that the subsequent learning is bound to be influenced by that sampling.

The *language tester* (who may of course in person also be the linguist and/or the language teacher) has the most difficult task of the three. In the first place, he or she must sample the learner's language behaviour in a very short time, often no more than three hours and sometimes less. Apart from the other individual variables (state of mind, health, motivation and so on) which may affect the outcome as in similar situations – for example, a job interview – there is also the ambitious claim that in the 3 hours or so available to a proficiency test the whole of the language is under scrutiny. In effect what the language tester must do is to negotiate a form of tacit understanding with the candidate that *most* language features and uses will not be tested (for example, local dialectal forms, archaic uses, high literary texts, recondite registers and so on). The tester is thus forced back inevitably to the position we outlined for the linguist and for the traditional language teacher, where what is tested in order to take account of as wide a range as possible is the more formal and the more rule-based, those concerns which are most likely to be generalizable.

In the second place, the language tester has to accept the burden of proof for his/her test in a way that is not required of the linguist or the teacher. In other words the tester is open to the demand that his/her test should be valid, that the most proficient learners should do best and the least proficient should perform least well; that the test should tease out the learners' errors and even that the test should indicate future learning both in the language itself and in other content subjects that are learned through the medium of the language. Such demands are heavy. They are not laid upon the linguist or the language teacher.

The linguist is expected to follow the internal requirements of scientific research and to ensure that his/her linguistic description should be economical, elegant and simple; the language teacher's materials, textbooks, pedagogic grammars, audiovisual materials, computer-assisted language teaching, realia *are* expected to represent the language, but the disagreements are likely to be only about the extent to which the texts chosen represent the language. Both the linguist and the language teacher are expected to meet the requirement of validity but in both cases it is an internal validity, whereas in the language tester's case the validity requirement is more extensive. In addition to meeting the demands of internal validity (including reliability), the language tester must also meet the requirement of external validity; that is to say, there is an absolute requirement that the most proficient learner should succeed in the language test, and vice versa for the least able. But the language tester's demands do not stop there.

Language teaching is programmatic (just as linguistic descriptions are to a large extent). We mean by this that they always hold something up their sleeves. The language teacher can always provide *another* example, *another* exercise, *another* text − and indeed it can be argued that a language teacher's success depends very much on his/her ability to do precisely this, to respond to the present context, a difficult response for many teachers who are not themselves native speakers of the language they are teaching. For the good language teacher therefore the textbook, the materials, whatever they are, are always and properly 'notes towards' rather than the complete dramatic script.

In the same way the linguist's description, the grammar, is rarely, if ever, complete. This is certainly the case with the more theory-driven descriptions, whether generative, functional, systemic, tagmemic or some other model, but it is even true of the large-scale descriptions, which tend to be more traditional, more eclectic. Always more can be added; always the grammar is a pro-legomena to a more definitive description.

Such is not the case with the language test. There we assume that the decision is final, that the 'right' learners are successful. And whether or not that is how we feel, the reality is that that is what happens since the selection is made, the candidates are aware (or not) of their results and the matter is ended. A language test cannot therefore afford to be programmatic, to indicate what it would be useful or interesting or important or even fun to do; what it must do is to represent a decision as to what has to be done and then to do it. Language tests operate, that is to say, much more in the real world than either the linguistic description or language teaching. Language tests, in other words are operational: they provide operational definitions of language behaviour and of adequate language behaviours, that is acceptable levels that are mean-ingful in some sense in themselves through determining appropriate cut-offs.

In this matter language tests distinguish themselves not only from language teaching syllabuses but also from examinations, though this *should* not happen. It is the case that examinations are sometimes constructed in order to try out a good idea and then if the idea does not work in the examining process (or if it is not clear whether or not it has worked) there has to be a rescue attempt to manipulate the unsatisfactory results. Language tests have to stand or fall by themselves. As we shall see, such a dichotomy cannot be maintained: tests do sometimes have examination features, such as the undesirable one we have just mentioned; equally, examinations are sometimes more rigorously prepared and attempt to build in some of the more objective features of testing. But it is useful for demonstration and argument purposes to behave as if the two forms of assessment were distinct.

Statistics in Language Testing

Many accounts of language testing quite properly deal in detail with the statistics needed (Allen and Davies 1977, Oller 1979). In this book we will take the statistics for granted, in the sense that while we recognize profoundly that language testing cannot be conducted without adequate statistics, we will accept that statistics are best taught through tuition and more focused textbooks (and increasingly, of course, through computer programs). Where necessary we will comment on the concepts required, but we will not attempt to teach any methods nor will we consider statistical formulae in any detail. We shall assume that the reader has access to adequate statistical understanding and, lacking that, help.

But we will comment here on the value of statistics in language testing and experiments. A distinction is often made between *descriptive* and *inferential* statistics: descriptive statistics are used to summarize a set of results, to give, for example, the average or mean and the range or standard deviation as the best simple summary of a whole array; inferential statistics are used to indicate to what extent we can accept the sample of cases (people or things) that have been tested or measured as representative of the population from which they are said to have been drawn; thus, to take a very simple example, if I give an English test to a group of French speakers and a group of German speakers then one of the questions I would be asking is to what extent the French and the German learners perform differently, belong statistically to different populations. If in fact there is no 'significant' difference between them then, while I cannot conclude that the French and the Germans are the same in every way, I can conclude that on this test (and therefore, by extrapolation, in English generally) they can be regarded as belonging to the same population and not to separate ones. Arguments of this kind which set out to test hypotheses about differences between learners and learning require inferential statistics for their resolution.

This comparison of the two main branches of statistics allows us to suggest further comparisons. In Table 1 we have put validity along with sampling under descriptive statistics. The connection we suggest here is that validity in testing concerns the same sort of requirements that sampling does in experiments. In an experiment (for example, a laboratory pharmaceutical experiment) in which it is crucially important that the materials under test should sample what they are supposed to sample as closely as possible, the drugs, the

Table 1.   Statistics and Testing Concepts Compared.

Descriptive	*Inferential*
Validity = Sampling (testing) (experiments)	Reliability = Significance (testing) (experiments)

patients, the treatments and the locations should all reflect exactly the real situations, so that the decisions can be made as to whether or not the products 'work'. Good sampling means being able to make such decisions, that is that if it works in the laboratory then it will also work outside and of course the converse, that if it doesn't it won't. Sampling in experiment means being true to reality and that is exactly what validity is about in language testing. Validity concerns – in different ways – being able to say: 'yes, this is a good test in this context and for this purpose. I know because of the sampling we undertook in constructing it.'

Under inferential statistics we have reliability and significance and again we make a link between them and, in doing so, propose a further relationship between testing and experimentation. The claim of significance in an experiment, we have already suggested, means being prepared to take a calculated risk that the experiment works, that according to the normal conventions other experimenters would agree with you if they carried out the experiment for themselves. Such a decision as to the amount of risk one is prepared to take depends substantially on a statistical argument and there are many ways of testing for this result. Reliability in testing also means being prepared to accept that the result, in this case the test, will provide an adequate measure which is reproducible. Testing quotes a figure for reliability just as an experiment will quote a figure for significance, and the user is then able to determine to what extent the test result (or indeed the experimental result) can be accepted. Just as there are conventions for the amount of risk-taking in an experiment, precisely what level of significance can be accepted, so there are conventions as to how much reliability is needed for a test to be regarded as satisfactory. We will return to validity and reliability.

Norm- and Criterion-referenced Tests

A test is normally a question or a set of questions, or a task or set of tasks. So of course is an exercise and indeed it is not always clear what distinction, if any, there is between a test and an exercise. We will suggest two basic differences.

In the first place a test establishes a rank order; an exercise does not. Here we are indicating what is, in our view, one of the fundamental purposes of a test, that a test is intended above all to clarify the differences in the matter under test, in what is being tested (proficiency, aptitude, achievement) among the candidates. Such a view is often said to reflect a *norm-referenced* view of language testing which imposes a normal distribution on those under test, whether or not such a distribution is there in reality. Opposed to this norm-referenced view is that of *criterion referencing*, which sets attainable targets and goals for those under test and is, it is claimed, more concerned with the nature of the task to be attained than with what separates individual learners.

Of course there are two underlying agendas here: one is philosophical—humanist and concerns moral views on whether in society it is ever right to differentiate among individuals in terms of abilities, or whether it is more democratic and fair not to do so. (Supporters of criterion referencing do, of course, accept that some learners will not reach criterion: that extent of differentiation is thought to be acceptable.)

The other agenda is more closely tied to language (since the moralistic view of criterion referencing extends to all education) and it concerns the validity of making distinctions among learners in terms of their language performance, on the grounds that there is perhaps no one obvious way in which communication can be observed. That being so, it is argued, it is supererogatory to pretend that there are real distinctions among individuals, real in the sense of being valid in terms of communicative use, and that all that we can do (all that we should do is of course a question for the moralistic view) is to make quite crude distinctions of above and below a line.

Interest in criterion-referenced tests has come, in part, from a greater interest in the whole question of curriculum development and partly from a distaste for the ranking function of tests. Ideally, criterion-referenced tests have the following characteristics: they test externally defined objectives, they test on a syllabus or content rather than on a rank order, they are used diagnostically, and they test all relevant behaviour, not just samples of it (Bormuth 1970, Brown 1981). Naturally there are difficulties in using criterion-referenced tests for language: there is no finite inventory of learning points or items; there are very many behavioural objectives; there are variable (if any) external criteria of success, of fluency, of intelligibility and so on; there is no obvious way of establishing adequate knowledge, of saying how much of a language is enough. As Cronbach (1961:335) has reminded us 'setting a cutting score requires a value judgement'.

Valette and Disick (1972) propose a model based on two claims: first, that criterion referencing gives a relevant and non-subjectively defined learning programme, and second, that it can be used to provide an individualized instruction programme. (It is useful here to link criterion referencing with the attempt at item and objective specification of programmed instruction in the early 1960s). In order to specify student learning objectives, Valette and Disick suggest an interrelationship of two performance objectives, formal and expressive, and two taxonomies, the subject-matter and the affective. It is, however, difficult to see how criterion-referenced tests can be constructed in a completely separate way from norm-referenced tests, that is without the usual canons of item discreteness and discrimination.

There is another way of looking at the two kinds of test. Most teachers are concerned with very small (and often quite homogeneous) groups of learners. What they require is a criterion-referenced use of a norm-referenced test, a test that does not discriminate greatly among their students but which does establish an adequate dichotomy (or cut-off) between plus success and minus success. If we accept this point of view, criterion-referenced tests are essentially special uses of norm-referenced tests with small groups. For every criterion-referenced test there must be a population for whom the tests could be norm-referenced. Criterion referencing is therefore more properly regarded as suitable as an exercise (a task that all the population can do, as opposed to a test − norm-referenced − which they cannot), or as a means of deciding on where to set a cut-off. Setting a cut-off may indeed require a value judgement but it is essential in order to establish how much of language learning is enough and therefore what is adequate proficiency. Neither use of norm referencing is new. Criterion referencing is a valuable and salutary way of looking at existing tests and reminding us that in a given situation we are always concerned with determining how much is enough. The work on the teaching of modern languages in Scotland in recent years, the Graded Levels of Achievement in Foreign Languages (Clark 1987), uses criterion referencing precisely in this way.

From our point of view a criterion-referenced test is one use of a norm-referenced test; but the argument is often presented as though criterion referencing were in itself a method of test construction. It is not. 'Underlying the concept of achievement measurement is the notion of a continuum of knowledge acquisition ranging from no proficiency at all to perfect proficiency. An individual's achievement level falls at some point on the continuum as indicated by the behaviour he displays during testing. The degree to which his achievement resembles desired performance at any specified level is assessed by criterion-referenced measures of achievement or proficiency.' (Glaser 1963:519)

In our judgement the arguments about criterion and norm referencing are somewhat metaphysical. Both types of test sampling (for that is what norm and criterion referencing are) need one another. Neither is usable alone. Norm referencing always at some point uses criterion referencing in order to determine a cut-off, a level that needs to be reached for some purpose. Similarly criterion referencing requires norm referencing in order to establish just what it is learners are capable of, what the best can do in a limited amount of time, and so on. The athletics analogy of the high jump (for criterion referencing) and the long jump (for norm referencing) is sometimes used and it is salutary to remember that even the high jump depends for the level that is set on previous knowledge of what athletes can achieve.

Acceptance of tests as basically norm-referenced requires that we accept that a test establishes a rank order. Having made that point categorically it is only right to repeat the point just made that there are of course situations in which rank orders may not be wanted. In language testing this is often the case in classroom testing where for various reasons (the task in question or the nature of the group) it is not sensible to produce a rank order. In such cases of course criterion referencing will be what is used; thus reinforcing the point already made that criterion referencing is best seen as one use of norm referencing.

It is for this reason that a test is not an exercise. While, by my argument, a test is meant (by definition as it were) to discriminate, to produce a rank order, an exercise is not so intended. The purpose of an exercise − again in institutional settings where learners are receiving class-based instruction − is to give practice to whole groups. That means that the task presented in the exercise must be within the capacity of all the learners; indeed an exercise which most learners could not do (or got 'wrong') would be inappropriate, whereas the same exercise used as a test could well be very appropriate if it was desired to test for a very difficult area of skill or knowledge. Tests allow for discrimination at chosen levels, exercises do not. And since we have just been considering norm and criterion referencing and making a similar distinction between them, it is appropriate to conclude here that testing is particularly suitable for norm referencing while criterion referencing is more easily exhibited in exercises than in tests.

Test Purposes and Uses

The main purposes of language testing are those of selection, feedback, evaluation and research. We are concerned with:

1   *selection* for more advanced courses and institutions;
2   providing for *feedback* to the syllabus so that there is some of that external validity for language teaching which I suggested earlier exists in language testing but not in language teaching;
3   the *evaluation* of materials and methods − an important but somehow under-used activity, perhaps because of the lack of agreement on how to begin judgement on materials or a project or methods since they are so often complete in themselves and can therefore be judged only in their own terms.
4   *experimentation*, where it is normal for measurement to be made during the experiment, and for further testing of a more specific kind to be carried out after the experiment is over in order to determine how meaningful ('significant') the results are. These topics are discussed more fully in chapters 7, 8 and 9.

We can distinguish four test uses: *achievement* (or attainment), *proficiency*, *aptitude* and *diagnostic*. The different uses can be distinguished in terms of time and content. Thus the *achievement* test refers back to previous learning and is concerned solely with that; achievement tests are typically used at the end of a period of learning, a school year or a whole school or college career. The content is a sample of what has been in the syllabus during the time under scrutiny.

The *proficiency* test is also interested in what has been learnt but in a much more vague way. Unlike the achievement test the proficiency test exhibits no control over previous learning; instead it establishes generalizations on the basis of typical syllabuses leading to entry and is more directly related to what it attempts to predict, namely, performance in the language under test on some future activity. (Examples might include English for medical doctors who will be working in Australia or for foreign students intending to study in American or British unversities, or Arabic for diplomats and so on.) It is usual for proficiency tests which achieve some measure of acceptance and institutionalizing to convert themselves into achievement tests. What actually happens is not a change in the test, but the development of a teaching programme related to the test. A course is set up towards the proficiency test which effectively converts the proficiency test into the achievement test of its now well-known syllabus. As we shall see, we can also distinguish test uses in terms of validities.

Unlike the proficiency test the *aptitude* test has no content (no typical syllabuses for teaching aptitude) to draw on but like the proficiency test it is concerned to predict future achievement, though this time not in language for some other purpose (for example, practising medicine) but in language for its own sake. An aptitude test is intended to predict future language learning success. Its design is, however, more problematic than that of either an achievement or a proficiency test since there is no body of skill or knowledge that can be sampled to produce an aptitude test. Instead it is usual to *model* aptitude (as a first step in theory building) and to test that model statistically through a method such as factor analysis. Typically, aptitude tests draw on such abilities as first-language verbal knowledge, ability to codify unfamiliar phonemic features, and motivation. None of these can be said to represent a body of content available to the learner.

Diagnostic tests are the reverse side of achievement tests in the sense that while the interest in the achievement test is in success, the interest in the diagnostic test is in failure, what has gone wrong, in order to develop remedies. There is also the more widely based diagnostic test which purports to provide a detailed profile of particular areas of language learning. The truth probably is that, except in speech pathology instruments such as the LARSP (Crystal *et al.* 1976), language testing does not really make use of diagnostic tests in this more accurate sense; there is often a hope that diagnostic tests will become available but they have not yet begun to emerge in spite of the computer-adaptive testing developments which in terms of speed and memory would seem to be the most suitable method so far of making diagnosis available to individuals. Indeed diagnostic testing is probably best thought of as a second stage after achievement or proficiency testing has taken place and as such its suitability for testing individuals suggests that it is better seen as an elicitation than as a test.

Reliability and Validity

We have mentioned the two concepts of reliability, concerning the consistency of test judgements and results, and of validity, concerning the truth of the test, its relation to what it is intended to test. It is usual to distinguish four methods of establishing reliability in a test: parallel forms (or versions) of the test; test–retest; split-half; and internal consistency.

In order to show the extent of a test's reliability the most obvious way is to construct an exactly similar version of the test, to pilot that on the same sample as the first version and then to compare results. A highly reliable test will have complete agreement (or very nearly so) between the two versions. Of course there are problems – such as ensuring that the sample under test is behaving in the same way at each test administration – but approximations can be made. The greater problem is to be sure that one test is in fact *exactly* similar to another and while this can be statistically achieved (through comparable item indices) there seems be no safe way in which we can be sure from a language point of view that one test item is equivalent to another. Here is an example of a matched item:

a.1. John lives in Paris. Where does John live? Answer:　.
a.2. John lives in Rome. Where does John live? Answer:　.

Even in such parallel items (a1 and a2) the difference between Rome and Paris may be enough to disturb candidates. What is more important, however, is the implication of this for more integrative testing; if exact parallelism is difficult even in such unidimensional items how much more difficult it is in more complicated tests.

A second alternative is to use exactly the same test and repeat it with the same subjects. The assumption here is that, while *all* subjects will do better because of practice, they will all do so equally well. That is an assumption that cannot be seriously accepted. A third alternative is to give the test only once but to behave as if it was in fact two tests, two versions, which happened to have been administered together. The test can then be split in half, the two halves correlated and then the correlation which indicates the reliability of one half can, through a straightforward boosting formula, be reinterpreted to show what reliability can be claimed for the whole test. The problem here is that there appears to be no principled way in which a test can be split in half.

The usual method nowadays – especially with computing programs for calculating test statistics – is that of *rational equivalence*, normally using the Kuder–Richardson formulas 20 or 21. It is usually suggested that the rational equivalence method (which is based on the number of items and the standard deviation) is in effect an averaging out of all possible split-halves. Reliability can be increased and improved by extending the length of a test: indeed it is possible to make any test highly reliable if made long enough, *given enough time* – which perhaps shows that reliability alone is somewhat vacuous. Another method of improving reliability is to emphasize homogeneity of test items, in itself a reminder of the basic function of reliability, to measure consistency.

Reliability is necessary for a test (it must have at least a correlation of 0.9, giving a consistency of 0.90 or 81%) but it is not sufficient. What matters in a test is that it should be *valid,* and in a moment we will discuss the various types of validity, but it is worth pausing for a moment to probe more fully the importance of reliability.

Being consistent in itself has no value, it may be argued, since it is possible to be consistent about trivia. And yet is this so? Since language tests are unlikely to be other than *language* tests and since, *pace* our earlier remarks about sampling, it is likely that all language behaviour is important, then that makes reliability out to be perhaps the most important single feature of a language test. The issue is of course not quite so simple and it is not possible to get away from validity since, as Bachman and Palmer (1982) have shown, there is a sense in which what may appear to be a test of a skill turns out to be a test of a method. For example, we may firmly believe we are testing reading comprehension on the one hand and listening comprehension on the other, when in fact what both are testing is technique in tackling multiple-choice tests. We conclude that we cannot allow reliability to dominate our thinking and we are compelled to agree that validity deserves its central place, but at the same time we must not go the opposite way and claim that reliability — because it says nothing about truth — is unimportant and we can therefore afford to let test reliability slip. That will not do either. Just as there is no point in testing something unimportant, so there is no point in testing something which is randomly — and therefore not at all — important.

Validity is often discussed under the headings: *face, content, construct, predictive, concurrent.* Let us take each in turn. *Face* validity concerns the appeal of the test to the lay judgement, typically that of the candidate, the candidate's family, members of the public and so on. Given the public nature of testing it is clearly important that a test should, if possible, contain face validity. However, if there is conflict between it and one of the other validities, then face validity must be the first one to go. Its importance is in public relations, but that does not mean it is unimportant since, as I have said, testing is a public, political type of activity, an acting upon the world.

Content validity on the other hand is a professional judgement, that of the teacher or tester. They rely on their knowledge of the language to judge to what extent the test provides a satisfactory sample of the syllabus, whether real (for achievement testing) or imagined (for proficiency testing) or of the theory or model (for aptitude testing). Here content validity slides into *construct* validity since it is as a sample of the theoretical construct that such tests as aptitude are constructed. That being so, it is difficult to keep content and construct apart except in terms of the test uses they most closely refer to.

Similarly, predictive and concurrent validity are closely related. *Predictive* validity has to do with the predictive force of a test, the extent to which test results predict some future outcome. One important use in recent years has been the attempts to make proficiency tests more valid by increasing their predictive power of future academic success of, for example, overseas students studying in the English medium in the UK, the USA and elsewhere. Prediction has to do with future outcome and therefore concerns a criterion that is not actually available at the time of the test, a criterion such as grades in an academic subject which is being studied through the medium of the language under test, or indeed success in a language course as a criterion of the prediction of an aptitude test. *Concurrent* validity on the other hand is based on a measure that is already at hand, usually another test, and in its most pure form concurrent validity can be established only when the test under scrutiny represents either a parallel version of the criterion test or a simplified version of it. No other comparison will do for concurrent validity. We put these various categorizations together in Table 2.

Table 2 Relation of Test Purpose, Use and Validity.

Test purpose	*Test use*	*Test validity*
Measure progress	Achievement	Content
Evaluate programme	Proficiency	Predictive/Concurrent
Investigate learning	Aptitude	Construct
Illumine syllabus	Diagnostic	Content

Practical Constraints

There are obvious practical constraints on language testing which affect its validity. Indeed attempts to make tests more valid can be seen as ways of trying to overcome these practical constraints.

Tests are typically receptive rather than productive. That is not to say that a productive test of speaking or writing is not possible, just that it is more difficult to construct reliably than a receptive test. It also has greater practical difficulties in that, for speaking tests, time and individual judges are needed and, for writing tests, there are problems of overcoming subjective impressions, however detailed the instructions may be.

Testing is not teaching and we can − and should − insist that the operation of testing is distinct from teaching and must be seen as a method of providing information that may be used for teaching and other purposes. However, the reality is that testing is always used in teaching, in the sense that much teaching is related to the testing that is demanded of its students. In other words testing always has a 'washback' influence and it is foolish to pretend that it does not happen. The kind of testing that is employed and the aspects of language that are tested necessarily find their ways into the teaching programmes: if grammar is tested, then it will be taught; if spoken language is not tested, it will not be taught; if reading comprehension of set texts is tested then that is what students will be exposed to − and they are likely to be exposed only to set texts and never to unseen texts. This is a heavy responsibility, especially for those who question face validity and who argue for indirect testing. Given the inevitability of washback the sensible thing to do is to accept it and make sure − or attempt to do so − that the feedback provided is beneficial, that it makes for satisfactory (valid and reliable) testing and, at the same time, that it provides for satisfactory teaching content and methods.

Since testing is, as we have observed, so influential in teaching there is a temptation to use testing as a quick way of influencing the teaching. The argument would be precisely the one we have just presented for feedback: that washback is inevitable, and we should therefore take advantage of it in a situation where change has been very slow. That is dangerous, because in itself the testing system cannot produce change quickly (see chapter 7). If there is a readiness for change then it is likely that the teaching (materials, methods) as well as the teachers and their training will also be ready for change and then all three elements, teaching, materials and testing, can operate together. But if either one has to be used to influence the others, the situation of imbalance is likely to produce failure of the attempted innovation.

There is also the most obviously practical problem which faces testing of all kinds, what Melville called the need for 'time, cash and patience', which in the present discussion means ensuring that the facilities, the materials, the personnel and so on needed for a new test are in fact available in the numbers and at the times they are required. For example, a test which requires individual oral interviews for a population of thousands of candidates all to be tested on the same day is likely to prove difficult if there is a shortage in the number of qualified and experienced interviewers. Tests which require both interviewers and interlocutors, or that all spoken interviews should be recorded, or that large numbers of individual test papers be provided for each candidate, or that a listening test should be presented in what turn out to be very noisy downtown conditions, are all likely to produce practical difficulties which need to be foreseen when the test is in process of development. In brief, a test should simplify as far as possible and limit its requirements of people, time and materials. Of course, in saying this, we are − as we have already observed − putting a strong constraint on the increase of validity.

Reliability allows us to overcome our doubts about the 'mere' arithmetic of a test result, that what we have done is only to add together a set of numbers which may or may not have much relation to one another − and which furthermore may often been achieved in quite different ways: for example candidates A and B may both have a score of 20 on a test containing 40 items but while A's 20 derives from items 1−10 and 31−40, B's score − also of 20 − derives from items 11−30. In other words, A and B share the same score and yet they may as well have taken different tests. But reliability at an appropriate level can guarantee that all 40 items are indeed connected − because what reliability (especially of the Kuder−Richardson (KR) internal consistency variety) demonstrates is that there is consistency about the test as a whole, that scores from any section of the test are equivalent to scores on any other section.

Content validity allows us to overcome our doubts about sampling. We may well feel uneasy about the language sample we have put together for a test but we can overcome that doubt by seeking the supporting judgements of other specialist professionals. Their agreement that the sample does indeed represent the language area under test allows us to rest easy on the sample we have drawn. *Predictive validity* is likewise a means of getting away from one's own subjective impression of a task and a test. We may feel torn by humanistic doubt about making judgements about other people in that the test we have constructed is, as we know better than others, full of error, and in any case how can a single performance be used to make important judgements about people's lives (for example, selection for scholarships)? The support we need here is the predictive validity of a test, because what that shows us is that our test judgement was in fact better than chance would have been. That is what a respectable (not a high but a respectable) predictive validity correlation means, that our testing judgement is better than chance would have been. Indeed it is probably the case that far more testing effort should be put into predictive validity, especially of proficiency tests. The present situation is that the predictive validity of such tests is rarely, if ever, very high (or even respectable) and one of the major theoretical (as well as practical) problems in the way of improvement is, as we noted in chapter 1, that we do not know how to improve the selection of criteria against which we typically measure a test's predictive validity.

3 Language Test Purposes

Three Questions

There are three questions about language testing fundamental to the argument of this book and basic to our understanding of the sources, the role and the construction of language tests. We now pose these questions, discuss them and consider solutions to them. The book is deliberately theoretical rather than practical, and sets out to provide a conceptual framework for language testing. The intention, as we have seen, is to place language testing firmly within Applied Linguistics, a position which it has swiftly come to occupy in the 15 years since the classic overview by Corder (1973).

The three questions are:

1 What is the relationship between language testing, linguistics and language teaching studies?
2 What value does language testing have in Applied Linguistics, in language learning and teaching, and in linguistics?
3 What does 'doing language testing' mean in the sense of the practical reasoning common to language testers, itself a product of professional training and experience?

Question 1: the relationship between linguistics, language testing and language teaching studies

Linguistics is, in the first instance, descriptive, seeking to answer the question: what? what is the nature of language? Language teaching and language learning are, again in the first instance, procedural, concerned to answer the question how? How are languages learnt and taught? There is no doubt that both linguistics and language learning/teaching are eventually concerned to be explanatory, to answer the *why* question: why is the structure of language or the acquisition of language like this? – but in our judgement this epistemological question is not a question within linguistics, it reduces linguistics to being part of philosophy or of psychology. Indeed, we have seen in the last 20 years claims from philosophers of language and from psycholinguistics that linguistics is really something else, has no substance in itself that requires it to be an independent discipline.

In addition to its primary theoretical responsibility, linguistics also has a secondary responsibility: to respond to the language learning/teaching question how? about, for example, structural relationships and their best fit. Equally, language learning and teaching have a secondary responsibility: to answer the question what? about, for example, the proper content of the order of acquisition or of a teaching syllabus.

Language testing is primarily concerned to answer the *what* question rather than the *how* question. Again of course it must do both, but it aligns itself, interestingly, in this context more with linguistics than with language teaching and learning. In other words, the first question about a language test is *what* to test and only then comes *how*, what methods to use to test what we want to test. As we shall see the *what* of language testing (as indeed of linguistics) includes its own *how*. The *what* alone implies a rigid (Saussurean) distinction between the synchronic and the diachronic views of language, between the still film and the movie, between outcome or product and process. Later we will take up this how process question and consider to what extent it is possible to require of language tests that they measure process as well as product. As we shall see, this issue involves a basic decision about the nature of language and raises the question of to what extent outcomes are determined by processes and, if they are, to what extent we will interpret *how* as being method-related only, and therefore view language testing as being first of all concerned with content, that is, what must be tested.

Question 2: the value of language testing

There is a later question which has to do with our motives for engaging in language testing as a useful activity. This is the question *why*? Why do we want to engage in language testing, what do we do it for? Now this is not really a question we ask ourselves about linguistic studies nor about language learning and teaching. It is, as it were, self-evident that studying linguistics is a justifiable activity. It is equally (perhaps more) understandable that language teaching and as its corollary the study of language learning — we are here of course focusing on the study not the activity of language learning — are proper studies and activities to engage in. Language testing is much less self-evident. Like the activity of language learning we may accept that the activity of language testing is something that happens, a sort of regular behaviour, but the discipline of language testing directs our attention to questions of explanation. Why do we test language? What is a language test for? And although that explanatory *why*? is not the primary question for language testing studies it is always the first question that the language test constructor must pose. This is the question of purpose and it really must be asked before we can resolve the content, the *what* issue. It may be, of course, that in any study, in any voluntary activity the *why* question is always the first one to answer even though it may be passed over and taken for granted. If that is so, then the first question of a language teaching programme is *why*, why is this language being taught in this situation to these learners, and only when we know the answer to these sorts of purpose questions can we decide what the programme should contain, the *what*.

Let us consider the *why* question for language testing further. There are two levels to it, the first is what we want to do with the information from the test. This is a question about the kind of test we will construct, achievement, proficiency, aptitude, diagnostic, and when this decision is taken the second question is *how* we propose to validate the kind of test we have chosen, which type of validity we appeal to, either separately or in some combination. We will argue that it is always necessary, except in special cases (for example with aptitude tests), to begin with content validity – and it is probably necessary to add to that either 'predictive' or 'concurrent'. We take this issue up later.

Question 3: what does doing language testing mean?

Language testing seeks to provide information. That information, in a large sense, may be what is required for some purpose where testing is used as an applied instrument, for example, to assess a group of learners; or it may be a research activity in its own right in which testing produces new data which may illumine language and language learning (and by implication language teaching). The view taken in this book is that language testing is a flexible and versatile endeavour which has a variety of uses but that at the same time that flexibility is constrained in two ways. First, by the demands of purpose: it is an absolute requirement that the language tester has already determined what information the test seeks to provide. As we have seen it is on that definition of purpose that the decision as to test content rests. Second, the flexibility is constrained by the necessary procedures and techniques that any testing activity demands. We have seen that these test construction procedures are largely statistical and practical and they are crucial if the language test is to be seen as a test.

The position we take then is that a language test has both language and testing requirements and it is to this combination of demands that any potential theory of language testing must address itself. As we shall show later, these twin demands can also be presented as the requirements of *validity* and *reliability* and we shall argue that both are necessary for serious language testing. Attempts to dismiss validity as an issue which does not contribute to test efficiency (as in less imaginative objective testing) or to dismiss reliability as a purely mechanical activity which has no language interest (as in more extreme forms of communicative testing) are both heretical approaches and must be rejected.

Language testing provides information: if that information is to be usable for teaching or for innovation (through experiment and research) then it must meet both the language and the testing requirements. Indeed, language testing is in a strong position within the language disciplines to meet these requirements, precisely because of the psychometric techniques which it makes use of and because of the test construction procedures it follows. Within applied linguistics language testing has arguably the strongest claim to rigour and falsifiability. From this point of view a test is a miniature experiment in that it 'proves' itself by virtue of its success in doing what it claims to do, that is, test achievement or aptitude. In addition, it incorporates methods of determining that proof. (Hence, of course, the increasing demand for testing as a necessary evaluation of language teaching programmes, a topic we take up in chapters 7—9.)

It has just been suggested that language testing is 'within applied linguistics'. When Pit Corder published 'Introducing Applied Linguistics' (1973) his view was that language testing existed on the periphery of applied linguistics. At the time that was a widely shared view. Developments in applied linguistics since 1973 have changed this view: the loosening of the dependence of applied linguistics on microlinguistics, the growth of second-language acquisition and interlanguage studies, the developments in language testing itself (Oller 1979, Alderson and Hughes 1981, Hughes and Porter 1983, Henning 1987, Bachman 1990) have led in the late 1980s to a view of applied linguistics which necessarily incorporates language testing as a central activity and component (see chapter 6). At the same time it is probably the case (though this is more difficult to substantiate) that those involved in language testing more often see themselves as applied linguists. It becomes increasingly important for postgraduate applied linguistics courses to contain a substantial element on language testing, including a sizeable statistical component.

This is, in part, a reflection of changes in *theoretical* positions so that our current view of Applied Linguistics now accommodates language testing in a more macrolinguistic view. It is also a reflection of the increasing demands of *professionalism* in language teaching which requires of its practitioners appropriate critical evaluation and assessment skills and knowledge in relation to the programmes they organize. Those skills and knowledge are within the domain of language testing.

Language Testing Information

What sort of *information* does language testing provide? We can distinguish 6 kinds.

The first is in *research* in which language testing is used to test hypotheses in relation to our understanding of language and language learning, particularly the latter. The status and concept of language proficiency, the structure of language ability (the 'unitary competence hypothesis', see below) and the natural order of language acquisition have been much discussed in recent years by language testers using language testing techniques to produce data which furthers discussion. Such issues are primarily intended to add to our knowledge and understanding of language and language learning, though no doubt they have an applied potential in language teaching programmes. These issues of language testing research are discussed in chapters 7–9.

A second use of language testing in *experiments* is to some extent a subset of our first use in research, since research uses experiments as a procedural technique. But there is an important difference. In the research use we are thinking of research into language testing; in the experimental use we are thinking of tests as criteria for language teaching experiments, for example in method comparison (Smith 1970, Beretta 1986; see also chapters 7–9). We hear less of such experimentation in the 1980s perhaps because of the particular problem of method experiments, and no doubt also because of the growth of small-scale experimentation is second-language acquisition research.

A third use which is *reflexive*, and though much discussed as a responsibility of testing is perhaps less used than it could be, is the *washback effect* on the syllabus of language testing. The implications of test results and their meaning are employed as a critique of the syllabus and the teaching; while the testing structure, content and method of the testing themselves face up to their inevitable responsibility of influencing the teaching. We are concerned here with the issue of teaching-to-the-test, for it is always the *pejorative* aspect of washback that is implied, but we again stress that there is a positive side to this. The implications are, first, that teaching is influenced by testing and, second, that testing has an important responsibility – to ensure that its influence is constructive.

The fourth use of language testing is *measuring progress* among learners, the most common use (the typical school or college examination is an achievement test).

The fifth is in *selection* of students on the basis either of previous learning or in terms of some more general language learning ability or aptitude for the next stage of education or for a particular vocation of some kind. What is of special interest here is the interaction between use for *progress* (no. 4) and use for *selection* (no. 5), that is, to what extent a valid test of progress is in itself a valid test for selection purposes.

The sixth use is in relation to *evaluation* of courses, methods, materials (not learners). Evaluation is on the increase and testing has a part to play. This is also a very special use of language testing which must cope with the learner variable, distinguishing it from the evaluation of the materials, programme, etc. It relates directly back to the second use, that of experiments, and is also discussed below in chapters 7–9.

As in other fast-moving disciplines much of the writing in the field of language testing is in papers and articles rather than in books. In all the social sciences (as in the theoretical and applied sciences) the emphasis is more on short accounts of research and the production of ideas; this is where applied linguistics firmly locates itself and, as part of applied linguistics, this is where we find language testing.

Over the past 25 years there have been a few major texts which are landmarks in the development and greater professionalizing of the subject. They are:

Lado, R. (1961); Valette, R. (1977); Oller, J.R. (1979); Alderson, J.C. and Hughes, A. (1981); Henning, G. (1987); and Bachman, L. (1990) – see References for further details.

Other influential texts noted in the References at the end of the book include: Jones and Spolsky (1975), Davies (1968), Allen and Davies (1977), Harris (1969), Heaton (1975, 1988), Carroll (1980), Hughes and Porter (1983), Portal (1986), Madsen (1983), Lee *et al.* (1985), Hughes (1989). In addition, the journal *Language Testing* has now been active for about 5 years and there are information circulars such as *Language Testing Update.* The development of language testing as a subject in its own right and as a core part of applied linguistics is thus supported and charted by this considerable body of scholarly activity.

Structuralist views and approaches deriving from structural linguistics were employed by Lado in his very successful book in the early 1960s (Lado 1961). As Quinn and McNamara (1988) point out, Lado's achievement in *Language Testing* (1961) was to interpret structuralist ideas and methods of analysis for the purpose of language testing, having already done much the same for language teaching. His ideas have continued to be of importance even though they have come under attack. In her book Valette (1967, 1st edition) attempted to extend to Modern European languages what Lado had successfully done for English as a Foreign Language (EFL). In the second edition (1977) she tried to move the discussion on (still in terms largely of Modern European languages) to notions about fluency and communication.

Oller (1979) took this discussion very much further. Indeed it might almost be said that Oller went *too* far too soon, in that he dismissed (by implication) communicative language testing for English Language Teaching (ELT) as being largely unrealistic and not pragmatic. He therefore advocated the types of approach which would earlier have been called integrative (notably cloze and dictation), arguing that such tests could test with simulated authenticity and at the same time retain high reliability. Oller's book is also important for its resurrection of the use of the statistical technique of factor analysis (see Alderson and Hughes 1981) in order to support his arguments about language ability, being himself an advocate of the unifactorial theory (see above). The logical development from Lado and Valette was not, or should not have been, into a book discussing pragmatic tests, but rather into more straightforward communicative tests.

Such a book has not been forthcoming and (with the two exceptions mentioned below) it may be that we have now accepted (as Oller would have us do?) that communicative testing on a wholesale model is too impractical to be realistic and that all testing has to be some form of compromise. The later books mentioned above have dealt with theoretical and technical issues. Alderson and Hughes (1981), has been influential in pushing on discussions about language testing as an applied linguistic activity, dealing with three fundamental topics in current language testing debate: the unitary competence hypothesis, communicative language testing, and testing language for specific purposes. Henning (1987), the most statistical of all the books quoted, deals in part with the uses of computerized technology for test construction and analysis, making use of item response theory (IRT), certainly one of the most important technical developments in recent years; indeed, it has been claimed it will revolutionize test construction (Masters 1982). Bachman (1990) deals, in part, again quite technically, with the technique of the multi-method/multi-trait procedure, a method for investigating test structure and therefore, as with the Oller use of factor analysis, the investigation of language ability.

We might repeat here that what has happened in the last 25 years is that language testing has moved its interest from the more practical to the more theoretical, from the more pedagogic to the more research-oriented. I comment below (chapter 6) on the dangers of such a development, but it is perhaps worth saying that, in general, all practice and pedagogy can only gain from greater theory and more research. This development in my judgement is, therefore, not bad in itself but it may possibly have a bad effect if, by emphasizing theory and research, it leads to a rift between practitioners and researchers.

The lesser known books can be divided into those dealing with practical matters: Madsen (1983), Heaton (1975, 1988), Harris (1969) and Allen and Davies (1977), and those dealing with more theoretical and research issues: Davies (1968), Hughes and Porter (1983), Portal (1986) and Lee *et al.* (1985). Two other books which deserve special mention are Carroll (1980) and Weir (1988). Weir's study is in part an attempt to present an account of the construction of a test of English for Academic Purposes (EAP) and does that satisfactorily. It is not, in spite of its title, a book about communicative testing except of course that English for Specific Purposes (ESP) is one part of communicative language testing (see below). Carroll's book is also not centrally about this subject. Indeed it is even more specialized than the other, in that what it is really concerned with discussing is the construction of a test for specific purposes. The problem with Carroll is that he makes out com-municative language testing, or its special brand of communicative language testing, to be far too easy, while Weir's informative discussion makes com-municative testing out to be a very daunting activity. We should also mention two other authors, Morrow (1977) and J.B. Carroll (1961). Morrow has made a very important contribution to the discussion by setting out in some detail and with eloquence the case for communicative language testing, and he has gone on to make a realistic and serious attempt to construct a test after his own blueprint in the Royal Society of Arts Communicative Use of English as a Foreign Language (RSA CUEFL). J.B. Carroll has had a great influence on the field both in his work on language aptitude with S. Sapon (1958) and in his theoretical discussion (based very firmly on empirical evidence) on the general questions of language ability and language learning.

The expected book on communicative language testing still waits to be written: in my view this is not now likely to happen given the time-lag, the loss of conviction about defining communication, and the sheer difficulty of the task. In the present book I discuss what seem to me important general issues about language testing and I hope to make it plain that language testing is firmly and rightly based in applied linguistics.

Important issues that arise in all discussions of language testing are: discrete point tests, integrative tests, criterion- and norm-referenced tests, production tests, communicative tests. These topics are all extensively surveyed in Davies (1978; see also Skehan 1988) but it will perhaps be helpful here if I indicate some of the main distinctions between discrete point and integrative, on the grounds that this distinction is a fundamental one in language testing (other definitions and distinctions are dealt with as they arise).

In testing, as in teaching, there is a tension between the analytical on the one hand and the integrative on the other. It is likely that 'progress' in language teaching consists of a dialectic between the two, indicated as a swing from the predominance of one emphasis to a predominance of the other. Thus in Spolsky's (1977) account of language testing development, the movement from Stage 2 (analytical) to Stage 3 (integrative) takes up no more than the decade of Valette's two editions (1967, 1977). Further, his Stage 1 (traditional) could well be regarded as a form of Stage 3, that is, as a kind of integrative or global view in which whole or real tasks of the kind of communication demanded are presented to the students, for example, translation or composition. Arguing that such tasks are not integrative or holistic is beside the point, since these activities have always been regarded by some teachers as what language teaching is for, the purposes and goals of learning.

As I see it, the most satisfactory view of language testing, and the most useful kinds of language tests, are a combination of these two views, the *analytical* and the *integrative*. It is probable in any case that no test can be analytical or integrative alone, that on the one hand all language 'bits' can be (and may need to be) contextualized; and on the other, that all language tests and discourse can be comprehended more effectively by a parts analysis. The two poles of analysis and integration are similar to (and may be closely related to) the concepts of *reliability* and *validity*. Test reliability is increased by adding to the stock of discrete items in a test: the smaller the bits and the more of these there are, the higher the potential reliability. Validity, however, is increased by making the test truer to life, in this case more like language in use. We can extend the distinction between analysis and integration to a series of similar and related distinctions, thus:

analytical	integrative
discrete point	holistic
norm-referenced	criterion-referenced
reception	production
linguistic competence	communicative competence

summative	formative
form	function
usage	use
idealization	raw data
deep structure	surface structure
language analysis	needs analysis
language sample	job work sample
competence knowledge testing	performance testing
indirect	direct
and we can add:	
reliability	validity

Compared with this major dichotomy the distinctions among test names such as aptitude, achievement, attainment, proficiency, diagnostic are of minor importance, since they do not have to do with the *nature* of language nor with a view of learning but with a particular test use (Davies 1978). Similarly, distinctions as to skill, such as oral, written, listening, reading and so on, are of less primary importance since they are again concerned with a mode of language or of learning transmission.

Oller (1976) puts forward a very strong claim on behalf of integrative tests: 'It is my opinion that so-called integrative tests are better than discrete point tests for precisely this reason' (1976:161) that 'the redundancy (or grammatical organisation) of verbal materials is a key factor accounting for a large portion of the variance in verbal experiments' and it therefore follows that 'language tests should invoke the examinee's capacity to utilize such organisational constraints' (1976:160). Oller includes among integrative tests 'cloze, dictation, translation, essay, oral interview' (1976:156). His claim here is expressed in the terms of his own speculations about a grammar of expectancy (Oller 1979), his term for the notion that prediction is the central element in language performance and that a test which captures that prediction is likely to be more valid than one that does not. Oller's argument then is about validity, that integrative tests are more valid than discrete point tests. Is this a necessary conclusion?

It is important to remind ourselves that discrete point tests are themselves typically intended for use in combination with one another in test batteries: it was always recognized that the sum of the whole was greater than any one of its parts. A test battery such as the Test of English as a Foreign Language (TOEFL), the English Proficiency Test Battery (EPTB), the English Language Battery (ELBA), the English Language Testing Service test (ELTS) gives a total score (in which certain parts may be weighted) and on one meaning of integrative this total score itself provides an integrated description of the testee's language ability. The other meaning of integrative, the view that Oller, for example, takes, is a Gestalt-type view which uses a performance-type task to assess performance. Further, it is Oller's claim that integrative tests such as cloze and dictation are not only more valid in themselves (performance tasks testing performance ability) but also that they contain greater validity than test batteries in relation to appropriate criteria. Oller's view here is extreme and has no doubt since been modified.

Over the past 20 years or so the writer has been involved, in varying ways, with three proficiency tests of English as a Foreign Language constructed in Britain. These tests are: the English Proficiency Test Battery (EPTB), the English Language Battery (ELBA), and the English Language Testing Service (ELTS) test. In all three cases the major concern was with validation. In chapter 4 I describe the experience of validating these three tests. In so doing, I have two purposes in mind. The first is for record purposes: the actual process of test validation is, as has been mentioned above, rarely described and discussed. What we hear about is the product of the validation, what the results are.

The second purpose is theoretical. The conclusion arrived at after this experience with proficiency tests and with validation is that construct and content validity matter above all. Of course it is the case that we can never be confident about individual test items until they have been properly tried out, but no set of items, however reliable, can improve upon an inadequate first analysis. What this suggests is, as we have agreed, that Anstey's first stage ('plan the content and general layout of the test...decide on the type of test item'; see chapter 2) is the crucial stage. It also suggests that the subsequent stages of test construction are essentially concerned with test reliability. If it turns out that a large number of trial items are unsatisfactory in terms of their item statistics (that is that they are non-discriminating or non-valid), what this means is that the *preliminary* analysis has been inadequate and/or rushed. Unsatisfactory items may also be produced by poor sampling of subjects undergoing the trials. The best safeguard against an unsatisfactory test is a professional job analysis at the outset, bringing together expertise in test construction and in language teaching. 'Job analysis' says Anstey (1966:24) 'can be carried out by an occupational psychologist in intimate cooperation with people with expert knowledge of the job. The psychologist should visit people at work on the job and preferably try it on himself for as long as he can spare before he starts forming any conclusions.' If we substitute 'language tester' for 'occupational psychologist' and if, as we have insisted, the language tester is a language professional as well as a testing specialist, then the language tester takes the place in Anstey's proposal of the occupational psychologist; furthermore, it is unlikely that the second part of the proposal ('The psychologist should visit...') will be required since the language tester will have previous experience of language teaching – but of course there are always new areas and levels of language teaching that he or she may need to find out about.

We argue in this book, therefore, that validity is central to language test construction and that the most important validities are content and construct. In the end no empirical study (to provide evidence for concurrent and predictive validities) can improve the test's validity (see chapter 4) – that is a matter for the content and construct validities. What is most important is the preliminary thinking and the preliminary analysis as to the nature of the language learning we aim to capture, Anstey's 'content and general layout of the test' (1966:59). While the procedures of language testing derive from psychological testing, valid language tests depend on test constructors' knowledge of language and on their judgement as to the parameters of language proficiency. The argument of this book is that language testing is an aspect of Applied Linguistics which is coherent in itself and has both a theoretical and a practical orientation.

4 Language Test Validation

Continuum Categories

Most test categorization is a practical matter. It takes account of test technique (for example, cloze, interview), of skill (oral tests, reading tests), of test uses (attainment, diagnosis) or even of particular learner samples (for example, norm- and criterion-referenced). The rationale for such taxonomies is that they provide a set of arrays for different purposes, they make the selection of a test possible and they also make it possible to find tests for many different purposes. What they do not do is to approach the fundamental testing issue, that of validity, directly. Validity (and its counterpart, reliability) is all too often added on to a test after it has been selected. What I want to suggest in this chapter is that test categorization can be usefully described in terms of three continua:

1 discrete point – integrative
2 linguistic competence – communicative competence
3 test – criterion.

I shall further suggest that these three continua can be located together under the superordinate of a fourth continuum, that of *validity*.

On the *first continuum*, the discrete point – integrative one (see Table 3), places are determined by the choice of discrete point or integrative mode for stimulus, task, item and scoring. In this continuum it is suggested that what distinguishes discrete point (DP) from Integrative (Integ.) items is the addition (or substitution) of test features of a DP or Integ. variety. The basis for this argument is the use of the design features of stimulus, task, item and scoring as way-stages along the continuum. Thus, a phoneme discrimination item is wholly DP. Relaxation of the DP approach at one point means that the phoneme discrimination item is no longer possible because the stimulus is now Integ. This argument depends of course on the assumption that reduction of the DP/Integ. constraint is progressive and sequential, that is, that the first loss of DP-ness has to be at the Stimulus point and cannot be at the Item point. What distinguishes for example 'cloze verbatim' and 'cloze acceptable'

Table 3. Discrete Point–Integrative Continuum.

Stimulus	*Task*	*Item*	*Scoring*	*For example:*
DP	DP	DP	DP	Phoneme discrimination
Integrative	DP	DP	DP	Reading comprehension
Integrative	Integ.	DP	DP	Cloze verbatim
Integrative	Integ.	Integ.	DP	Cloze acceptable
Integrative	Integ.	Integ.	Integ.	Essay

is Item since for cloze verbatim there is only a Yes/No item while for cloze acceptable Item is (almost) open-ended. And so on.

In the *second continuum*, that of linguistic–communicative competence, points are located in terms of the presence or absence of the twin features of validity and reliability. Table 4 sets out this relationship.

In this continuum items which are DP tests of linguistic competence lack validity (V) while items which are DP tests of communicative competence contain both validity (V) and reliability (R). This may look like special pleading. Certainly it assumes that communicative competence is basically 'better' than linguistic competence and that DP is better than Integrative. The best tests, on this basis, have linguistic competence (for reliability) *and* communicative competence (for validity). This is not entirely absurd.

Table 4. Linguistic Competence–Communicative Competence Continuum.

	DP	*Integrative*
Linguistic competence	−V +R	−V −R
Communicative competence	+V +R	+V −R

My *third continuum* (see Table 5) is that between test and criterion. It can be seen that an oral interview task will be further to the right, towards criterion, than a vocabulary or a grammar test. But there is a trade-in factor here in that tasks which are most criterion-like are least test-like; and since the purpose of testing must be to provide predictive reliable information, the further away from test-like tasks the less reliable that information becomes.

Table 5.   Test–Criterion Continuum.

Test	*Criterion*
tasks (test-like)	tasks (test-unlike)

Equally, the information must be true to the criterion and cannot afford therefore to be only test-like; in so doing it loses validity. Good tests are likely to be compromises between an emphasis on test-like and criterion-like qualities in the tasks they set.

In some recent discussions, as we shall see, it is not always clear that this distinction is maintained. A test is always a simulation of some kind for it cannot in itself realize the criterion which, by its nature, is difficult of access and uncertain. Tests and criteria are mutually supportive, and if we were able in an ideal situation to go to the criterion directly, we would then require a further criterion to validate our first. Thus the 'best' tests are likely to be compromises, placed at positions on one continuum which do not lead to unsatisfactory positioning on the others. Decisions as to locating on each of the three are of different kinds. The discrete point–integrative has to do with the test frame, the linguistic–communicative competence with the ability and the process, and the test–criterion with the reality or the authenticity of the context. It is difficult to bring all these qualities into one test item or one test, and that is a good reason for amassing information by combining test items (and indeed subtests) in order to sample the field. Notice that this is also an argument against the normal methods of item selection and item analysis which require homogeneity among items as the chief reason for selection or retention of an item, a demand that has rarely been made for selection or retention of subtests.

By way of illustration, let me turn now to a discussion of one oral test, the speaking component in the ELTDU–OUP Stage G test which forms an integral part of the ELTDU Stages of Attainment Scale (ELTDU undated). What this package does is to provide both a set of purposes which are objective and spelt out, and also tests for these purposes. (At least this is how it looks at first glance). The distinction I have just made between test and criterion is thus maintained, the purposes being the linguistic realizations tied to those purposes. I appreciate that the criterion of 'purposes' is not a complete one in that it depends itself on external validating for further support. This is inevitable: what it indicates is that no criterion is ever final — there is *no true criterion*, no apocalyptic revelation. Furthermore, it indicates that the validation of the 'purposes' is more an issue for the syllabus and the teachers than for the test. Eventually the tester has to put his cards on the table and become accountable in validity terms for the criterion he has selected. So in this case the test is validated against the criterion of the purposes and they depend on the tester's judgements. It will be noticed that this admitted uncertainty is also an argument for different validity supports, construct, content and predictive–concurrent.

The 'purposes' of the Stages of Attainment Scale are a series of stages of attainment. These are similar to more traditional placement of entry level descriptions. However, they are not in themselves bits of linguistic form but specifications of functions and they do not describe what the learner does or can do but what the stage or level requires of him. They are thus a kind of needs (or demands) analysis. They relate therefore to the van Ek (1980) and threshold level analysis and to the Munby lists (1978). In detail the specifications of the Stages of Attainment Scale relate to the uses of English in business: 'This Scale is intended to be used in business, companies and similar concerns in which information is frequently required on the language ability of personnel performing various functions throughout the company. This information may be required in order to know if, for instance, an employee can be sent to an English-speaking company, if he or she can meet an English-speaking visitor, or if the employee can write certain types of letters in English' (page 1). We are given step-by-step instructions on how to use the scales in the Administrator's Section and a Broad Description of Stages. We are then given a list of the various skills. Examples of those related to Listening and Speaking are:

Face to face dealings with customers, suppliers, agents

Dealings with visitors

Attending conferences, seminars

Verbally relaying information

Training

Making public statements

Use of the telephone

Ancillary and office services (typing, translating, interpreting)

Entertaining and other social purposes.

As will be obvious, here is one of the weak points in the system: why *this* set of functions, uses, rather than any other? Another weak point is the matching of the category of function to the task, and indeed the very specifications of the task. It is not easy to state in general terms 'the tasks(s) the employee is required to carry out in English'.

In addition to the Administrator's Section listing the Scales of Attainment there is a Teacher's Section which 'relates the levels of English defined in Section 1 to specific linguistic information on which teaching programmes and language assessment can be based'. The Teacher's Section provides the following information at each stage: 'A list of tasks an employee may be called upon to carry out at the given stage in both listening–speaking and reading–writing. A specification of the language necessary for carrying out the given tasks.' The van Ek model is quoted as the source for the approach followed. The stage I want to look at in connection with speaking tests is the highest but one, Stage G. Here the list of tasks is as follows:

'Employees should be able to:

Train native speakers without experiencing language difficulties.

Appreciate all the attitudes represented by the tone of voice of a native speaker.

Take the lead and guide a discussion no matter how difficult or sensitive the nature of the discussion.

Lead negotiations.

Conduct business over the phone.

Utilise a sufficient range of language to handle delicate or complex situations.' (page 68)

The language is not specified; indeed that attempt was abandoned at Stage F. Instead we have further uses and sub-categories of function suggested, for example:

At this Stage the emphasis is on training the employee to develop his language skills rather than on teaching any substantial body of new language. Training at this Stage should be regarded as a continuation of the elements outlined in Stage F: the employee develops his awareness of the possibilities of expression which can be conveyed by turn of phrase, intonation, gambit and so on. The skills of collocation, connotation and writing are developed in such a way that the learner increases his ability to use a wide range of communication acts in extended discourse. Oral comprehension and reading are trained according to the areas distinguished in Stage F, to a level at which the employee can perform the tasks required of him. (page 69)

The test component consists of three 'stage' tests, for levels C, E and G. It seems to be the case that one of the uses of the tests is to allocate students to the correct level of attainment. How this is done is not clear and it is at this point that for me the tests become unsatisfactory, a teaching device rather than a testing instrument. The elaborate specifications continue. The candidate is given a choice of three topics to discuss with the examiner and time to consider them. Then in an Elicitation Phase the candidate elicits from the examiner the information he or she requires. Finally, in the Summary Phase the candidate presents his summary of the chosen topic. Marks are allocated for both Elicitation and Summary phases, two kinds of mark in each case, one for Detail (articulateness, accuracy, tone. appropriateness and precision, comprehensibility, comprehension and assimilation, reciprocity), and one for Impression. The Impression marks are specified by letter and number (A = 11−15, B = 6−10, etc.). The Detail marks are left to the examiner.

While each phase is in progress the examiner should note positive and negative features of the candidate's performance against the categories set out in the mark sheet. *The precise way* in which these notes are made is *left to the examiner*, as they should convey to him significant points he wishes to remember. (*my italics*) Finally the notes made in the course of each phase against the categories should be used to decide a final mark within the impression grade awarded. (page 40)

Each candidate thus receives a Final Mark. It is, as will be understood, not clear either how to reach these Final Marks or what exactly they mean. What can one do with an A = 11−15 or an E = 0−5? The whole concept of this testing package as a test disappears, which is a pity because at first sight it looked promising, as a way of tying in the test with the criterion. Indeed it is, I fear, simply another listing of functions (useful enough for teaching and subjective judgements) and a judgemental scale which is of even *less* value than those numerous rating scales which at least suggest what a letter or a score mean.

How can we categorize this test in terms of the three continua I began with? In terms of the first (discrete point−integrative) it is located on either level 4 or 5, it depends on whether we call the scoring method discrete point or integrative. In terms of the second (linguistic competence−communicative competence) it is located firmly in the bottom right-hand cell, plus V and minus R. That is a charitable view. Others might want to put it in the top right-hand cell. In terms of the third continuum, that of test−criterion, I suggest that this instrument is much too far over to the right, too near the criterion, though not finally there. Perhaps all three continua can in fact be reduced to one, the central test criterion, that of *validity* on the continuum validity−reliability. Where this test appears on that continuum has already been pointed out in relation to the second continuum.

Types of validity can be related, as we have seen, to test uses, with the exception of face validity which relates to all test uses or to none. It is a truism to say that face validity is desirable but not necessary, cosmetic but useful because it helps convince the public that the test is valid. Content validity relates obviously to achievement (or attainment) tests in that the achievement test is deliberately constructed as a sample of the syllabus and materials. That being so, the content validity of the test is only a special case of the content validity of the syllabus, one is parasitic on the other. Note that there is a cumulative tendency with types of validity in their relation to test uses: an achievement test should have *both* face and content validity. An aptitude test should have face *plus* content *plus* construct validity and a proficiency test *all* three *plus* predictive concurrent validity. Aptitude tests are peculiarly dependent on construct validity because they do not sample in any obvious way past learning and are concerned wholly with future learning strategy. Hence the need for construct validity, that is to say, for theory.

Proficiency tests are sometimes regarded as tester's tests in that they must be free standing with no parasitism. But in order to stand up for themselves they require the support of the two types of validity which are typically established statistically: concurrent and predictive validities.

Both concurrent and predictive validity may make use of the same type of measure, experts' judgements rated on a scale (in language teaching usually teachers' judgements), another language test, an institution's language examination, or some academic or professional examination grade in the learner's subject area in which the medium is the language under test. Language test validity studies have frequently used academic grades in this way as a criterion (Davies 1984b) but it is not clear how justified this is. Although language enters into all our activities, how much it does so is not known. Certainly possession of language fluency does not guarantee academic success as academic differences among native speakers illustrate. The evidence when such academic criteria are used in language test predictive studies is not very persuasive: the typical correlation (Pearson product moment) is 0.3, that is, the variance accounted for between test and criterion is only 9 per cent.

As we have seen, the terms 'examination' and 'test' are sometimes used in free variation but they are also used to describe different kinds of measures: the test more standardized, more objective, providing norms and quoting reliabilities; the examination often more subjective, ranging from the careful design of, say, the Cambridge Proficiency Examination to the somewhat ad hoc one-off university or college end of year/session examination which may consist largely of open-ended essays. These require to be evaluated by carefully moderated scoring procedures and pooled assessments. In the British system the term examination is used even when long preparation and thought have gone into the design.

Three Levels of Validation

I want to consider now levels of test validation (from internal to external) as another type of continuum. To do so I present first three levels of validation of EFL examinations.

Validity 1   appeals to the internal logic of the system by setting up a series of examination levels, each one leading into the next (rather like a series of musical instrument performance grades). No doubt this is a commercial-type bid for a section of the language teaching market such that, if learners enter at the bottom level they are likely to continue in the same system. But its appeal is not only commercial since learners (and their teachers) are rightly attracted by the existence of a set of interlocking levels. It offers the feeling of confidence that the area has been surveyed and its territory mapped so that to move up the levels (for example, the Cambridge, Royal Society of Arts, Trinity College examinations) is to be demonstrating the learning of English. What Validity 1 is doing, after all, is claiming that sampling has taken place across the language.

Validity 2 is the acceptance of a new examination as the equivalent of an existing measure by demonstrating that it possesses both content validity and connection with a prestigious institution. This is common among EFL examinations. There must be content validity, that is the specialists must be satisfied when they look at the examination that it consists of the right bits, units, combinations, that it is, in other words, a test of what it says it is. When a new test is under construction, there must also be a prestigious institution with some involvement to provide credibility for the acceptance of the new examination. Finding a gap in the market is not easy — in their different ways the Cambridge Preliminary Examination, the Royal Society of Arts Communicative Use of English Examination and the AEB Test of English for Academic Purposes have tried to do this, illustrating that the problem exists even for well-known organizations. We may feel indignant about the power of success and the difficulty of newcomers making themselves known but from another point of view what prestigious institutions can provide, as in Validity 1, is confidence and a sense of consistency: these are important qualities in measurement.

Validity 3 is the appeal to an external criterion which I have already mentioned. Such appeal to concurrent and/or predictive validity through statistical analysis is done as a matter of course for tests but not for examinations. There is no reason why EFL examinations should not make use of some of this statistical apparatus; given the care and attention often put into their preparation it is wasteful not to carry out statistical analysis on them.

Validating Three Proficiency Tests

The process of validation can best be illustrated with studies I haved carried out on three EFL proficiency tests which I have been associated with (Davies 1984b). First of all the English Proficiency Test Battery (EPTB). This was a test I constructed on behalf of the British Council in 1964 to test the proficiency in English of overseas students coming to Britain for further studies. This test went into four versions up to 1977. The concurrent and predictive validity studies carried out on EPTB demonstrated that one minimum level of English proficiency could be regarded as adequate, whatever candidates intended to do with their English. The cut-off established by expectancy tables was low at the start but because of the inevitable regression to the mean it became necessary to raise the cut-off over time. I justified this one minimum cut-off by arguing that all students going through an academic course require a minimum language proficiency for studying in English medium in Britain, and thereafter what they need is ability and knowledge in the subject of their study. English proficiency then was regarded in terms of the EPTB as necessary to academic success in the UK, but in no sense sufficient. In other words a very weak claim was being made about the predictive validity of language in academic performance.

The English Language Battery (ELBA), designed by a former colleague Elisabeth Ingram, had much the same design features and raised a different though related issue to that of EPTB in the long-term study we did of ELBA's predictive validity – we used seven years of data from testing all overseas students (over 1600 in total) at entry to Edinburgh University (see chapter 9). ELBA results provided two findings of relevance to this discussion: first, that such validation studies are very difficult because of the criterion inaccessibility we have discussed above – supervisors and tutors are very reluctant to return a simple questionnaire asking for language proficiency information on their students. The second finding was that differential levels of English may be required for different types of academic study; in three Faculties (see Table 6) these were the combined mean scores of successes and failures on ELBA (success and failure referring to academic success/ failure in the students' academic courses in the university).

Table 6.   Mean Scores on ELBA by Faculty.

Faculty	Mean successes		Mean failures	
	Score	N	Score	N
Arts	78	278	70	5
Medicine	72	112	67	10
Science	64	141	53	7

The numbers of failures were (as they typically are) small but it is clear that Arts requires a higher mean than either Medicine or Science. Indeed Arts were failing students on scores (mean of 70) which would have indicated success in the Science Faculty (mean of 64). The conclusion that what matters for adequate performance is not the same for different Faculties is illustrated by the Successes and Failures figures, but while the differential Success figures suggest that the difference is one of levels (Arts needs more English than Science) the Failure figures may suggest that it is not only level but kind of English that distinguishes. The Failure numbers are very low but nevertheless the lack of difference *within* Faculties between Failures and Successes along with the cross-over imbalance for Failures and Successes *between* Faculties suggests that there may be a Faculty effect in proficiency differences. ELBA like EPTB was not designed to demonstrate different kinds of English for different subject areas but these results, however inadequate, raise this possibility, a possibility that the English Language Testing Service (ELTS) embodied as part of its original design.

A third validation study followed, this time on the English Language Testing Service's test (ELTS), the current British Council testing operation, taking over in 1980 from the EPTB which was used by the British Council for about fifteen years. The ELTS test is built on ESP principles: it contains general tests and a choice among six subject area modules. In our long-term (four years) ELTS validation study we compared ELTS with EPTB and ELBA in terms of concurrent validity, but the major part of the study was predictive and there we accumulated subject cases, that is, data from students taking the test, and then collecting also their academic grades and the proficiency judgements made on them later in their studies by their directors, advisors and supervisors (Criper and Davies 1988).

From the point of view of validation procedures the ELTS study was conventional in all ways except one. This exception was that we retested on ELTS towards the end of the students' first year. Most ELTS takers in the UK universities are postgraduates and many of these stay for only one year. As was noted earlier the predictive strength of an English proficiency test is commonly low, with a correlation of about 0.3. We have asked ourselves whether this is because our English tests, our predictors, are unreliable or otherwise inadequate; or because second-language proficiency really does play a very small part in academic success; or is there some other reason? It is possible that prediction necessarily decreases with time such that between the first testing with the English proficiency test (usually September/October) and the collection of academic performance scores at the end of the first year (at the earliest June but sometimes not before November), individual learning, differential learning, takes place which necessarily depresses correlations as the rank order of the predictor variables changes, since students' English develops more for some students than for others. We therefore hypothesized that it was this third possibility that made most sense, since we could not accept that language proficiency plays only a trivial part in academic performance and since the test instrument appears to be reasonably satisfactory.

Our expectation was that the correlation between the second ELTS testing and the academic criterion would be significantly higher than between the first ELTS test and the criterion. It was not. We achieved a non-significant result and could not therefore reject our null hypothesis. We are forced to accept that we have no evidence that causes us to claim that predictive validity is higher than 0.3, and we therefore need to explain why it is that language plays so small a part in academic study, only about 10 per cent of the variance.

The conclusion is after all one of relief: ten per cent is probably as large as it should be. Why? Because language must only be an entry into cognition and knowledge. It is in fact a useful finding in its failure to support the Whorfian hypothesis. Out of negative may come something of value after all! If language played a larger part, as we had always assumed, that would be tantamount to insisting that cognition is largely language-based, which is surely confusing the medium of cognition with the substance. That is not an attractive proposition, especially as it would argue for different cognitions across languages.

The process of validation can also be considered in connection with *project evaluation* where language tests are used to examine the validity of project claims. One such project which we have recently evaluated is the Bangalore Communicational Teaching Project in South India (Prabhu 1987). Descriptions of the Project and of the evaluation are given in Brumfit (1984a) and Beretta and Davies (1985). The Communicational Teaching Project was based on the view that children learn a second language by seeking for meaning and thereby acquiring the necessary language in order to secure that meaning, that is, to communicate. In other words communicating causes language learning and not the other way round. The Project went on for some five years in a number of Tamil- and Kannada-speaking schools in South India. Our task was to compare project classes with traditional classes (those taught on the usual South Indian structural syllabus). To this end we decided on a package of achievement tests for each class (to assess learning on the class's own method) and proficiency tests (to assess learning of English neutral as to method).

What we found was that each class did significantly better on its own method tests, the achievement tests; on the three proficiency tests, where there were any significant differences the Project classes did better. We concluded that there was modest support for the Project's view that grammar can be learnt through communicating and that grammar is deployable. We realized of course that our evaluation was heavily dependent on our proficiency tests being true proficiency tests and not disguised Project achievement tests. For the purpose of the present discussion what is of interest is the problem of constructing proficiency tests which are truly neutral. (A fuller account is given in chapter 7.)

The Superordinate Continuum of Validity

My final approach to validation processes is by way of these three quotations from Anastasi (1961) and Cronbach (1961):

(a) Correlations between a new test and previously available tests are frequently cited as evidence of validity. When the latter is an abbreviated or simplified form of a currently available test, the latter can properly be regarded as a criterion measure......unless the new test represents a simpler or shorter substitution for the earlier test, the use of the latter as a criterion is indefensible. (Anastasi 1961:145)

(b) ...desirable to retain the concept of the criterion in construct validity...to refer to independently gathered external data. The need to base all validity on data. . . Internal analysis of the test, through inter-test correlations, factorial analysis of test items, etc. is never a substitution for external validation. (op cit:151−2)

(c) The test constructor is not expected to answer every last question about validity before publishing his test, but he is expected to give the test user a fair impression of its validity. (Cronbach: 1961:107)

Both writers emphasize the need in all testing to assemble evidence; speculation must lead to empirical data collection, both are necessary. This is another way of claiming that *both* content or construct validity *and* concurrent or predictive validity are needed in the process of test validation. *Combining validities strengthens overall validity.*

We now present a validity matrix (Table 7) as our *fourth continuum category*, using the two dimensions of strong−weak and internal−external. First we consider this fourth continuum on its own, and second as imposed on our three earlier continua on the reasonable assumption that the dominant continuum in all considerations of language testing must be that of validity. Validities 1, 2 and 3 here refer to our earlier three levels of validity.

Table 7.   Validity Continuum Category.

	Internal	*External*
Weak	Validity 1	Validity 2
Strong		Validity 3

Notice that this leaves empty our fourth category, that of Internal/Strong, suggesting perhaps that internal validity must always be only weak by itself. This may indeed be the case for proficiency tests, but what about aptitude tests? They are, as we have seen, necessarily validated in terms of content and construct validity. Does that mean that an aptitude test cannot have strong validity? The answer surely is that it can, but that in order to do so it must have in addition to internal validity, external as well. This is true of, for example, the Modern Language Aptitude Test (MLAT) and we should therefore wish to say that the MLAT has Validity 3. We do not therefore need a fourth 'Validity 4' category.

Now to the imposition of this fourth continuum on our other three continua. Table 8 suggests that it is possible to relate all four continua and at the same time that the validity matrix is dominant, while the others are best seen as determinants of validity. The most favourably placed of all our entries is 'Test', in the sense that in the case of properly constructed tests, the other elements are already present. A test contains strong validity, it uses external support in its validation, and it seeks satisfactory reliability. As we have seen,

Table 8.   Four Combined Continuum Categories.

	Internal		*External*
Weak	DP	Linguistic competence	Criterion
Strong	Integ.	Communicative competence	Test

the underlying distinction in all our continua is that of validity−reliability. That is what distinguishes communicative and linguistic competence; equally what distinguishes integrative and discrete point items; and finally what distinguishes the criterion and the test. We have argued that in all cases compromise is required; that no test can ever be wholly valid or wholly reliable. Indeed, a completely reliable test would measure nothing; and a completely valid test would not measure.

5 Uncertainty and Explicitness

The Relation of Reliability and Validity to Uncertainty and Explicitness

A language test is a measure of language ability: it involves *language* and *measurement*, and it brings them together in order to define *ability*. All three elements, however, are inexact. It is necessary to remind ourselves that language testing is not an exact science, that it does not pretend to be precise. Indeed, its necessary and admirable attempt to be explicit about language, about measurement and about ability reveals how vague those areas are.

Language is used everywhere for communication between persons and for individual thinking. It is acquired early in life as part of natural child development but we know how difficult it is to distinguish language from other aspects of communication or from other forms of thinking. It is even less easy to pin down language if we look at it from a linguistic point of view, for from that point of view what matters about language is that it changes, changes over time and changes from place to place and from group to group. Indeed this process of change is so powerful that there is no *linguistic* argument for setting up determinate boundaries between people; in other words *languages* as discrete systems disappear, are deconstructed, because everyone speaks differently from everyone else. Language variety, the spatial aspect of the temporal language change, reminds us of the fugitive nature of language, above all of contemporary spoken languages which resist explicit description. However, language testing requires precisely such definition and carrying it out runs the risk of objection on the grounds of the 'language' not being properly or adequately presented. The 'language' has got away in such cases: language, like all human behaviour, is inexact (Davies 1988a).

Measurement: if we apply the principle of uncertainty then all measurement, even the most rigorous scientific measurement, lacks absolute precision. How much more is this the case in less exact sciences, particularly in the social sciences where sampling, significance, probability and confidence limits are all used to provide support for the imprecision of the measure. There are no true scores accessible although some are more true than others and it is the more-true-than-others that must satisfy us in our search for precision. Such uncertainty is characteristic of the social sciences, including those concerned with language. In psychometric testing the concepts of validity and reliability are invoked, as we have seen, as ways of determining what confidence we have in a test: *reliability* to provide the statistical reassurance of consistency of result, and *validity* to demonstrate that what is being measured thus consistently is in some sense important or real.

Important is used here in both senses, first as real − the test must relate however indirectly to the language behaviour that it claims to represent, thus an oral test must have some connection with the spoken language and a reading test must connect with reading skill and performance. The second sense of important implies non-trivial: thus a reliable and real test of memory for car registration numbers is unlikely to be valid as a language test because it would be trivial. A continuing criticism of language tests is that they emphasize *method* at the expense of *content*: thus, it is claimed, two multiple-choice tests of reading comprehension and listening comprehension may in practice be tests of multiple-choice skill and therefore similar because of the method instead of different (or at least possibly different) because the content or the traits are different. Measurement of language relies on acceptable degrees of reliability and standard error, which inevitably indicate an area of uncertain obscurity rather than a single point of brilliant certainty.

Language ability: there are two main senses of language ability. The first is the more general sense in which we make distinctions in terms of knowledge or performance. Even among native speakers we consider some people more fluent than others, better speakers, more effective writers, more efficient readers and listeners and so on. Such distinctions relate to norm-referenced judgements on the basis of which we regard all language ability as normally distributed. The second sense is more often used in relation to second- or foreign-language learners: here we take account of some level of native-speaker ability to which we relate the performance of second-language learners. Such an approach may be called criterion referencing.

The criterion in this case is a chosen level of native-speaker ability and that construct determines the goal (or criterion) we set for learners. What level of measured ability we accept as adequate for learners, what cut-off (or cut-offs) we accept as adequate, is a secondary and empirical question. We observe once again that in both cases, the goal and the accepted level, there is substantial uncertainty. Defining native-speaker ability is problematic as our reference to the imprecision of variety suggests; stating an appropriate cut-off is equally inexact since individuals must vary absolutely in terms of how much ability they require for different purposes and in different situations. Tests are constructed to measure kinds of ability, achievement, proficiency, aptitude. Such labels refer to areas of ability which they seek to capture but they do so only in some unclear representational or iconic manner.

Our construct of language ability is inevitably partial and our explicit realization of that construct in a language test is further removed from true performance. Mental skills can only be indirectly described: the attempt to capture them quantitatively in a language test is even more vague.

What we have been saying is that testing in the social sciences is prone to error and that this proneness is even greater when the content of the test is language. It is as though our very attempts to measure language founder not because our instruments are blunt − though they are − but because of the uncertainty of what is under test, language. What is needed is an acceptance of the relevance of idealized and theoretical models of language variety and standard language.

Language testing compels *explicitness* about language, about language learning, language teaching, language performance. It forces us to be clear about the aims and the content of our teaching, our syllabuses, our materials and our methods. It requires us to spell out in detail language criteria, language needs and language levels − not merely so that we can judge whether they have been met or reached but also so that we can explain to others and ourselves what we mean. Language testing operationalizes subjective judgements and in so doing both clarifies and validates them. But the explicitness of language testing − we have called it its main value − exacts a price, the price of *uncertainty*. Language tests do not provide exact information, it is always 'more' or 'less' and 'within confidence limits'. It is important to recognize that uncertainty from the start, to accept (and later describe) it and then to welcome it. For the sake of explicitness, for the information (though inexact) it provides, for the demand it makes to examine and re-examine our assumptions about language and our decisions with regard to language planning, language policies, language teaching and language certification, for all this, uncertainty is a low price to pay.

Language testing is mainly about these two things: *being explicit* as to what is being tested and what has been learnt and *controlling uncertainty* through statistical operations. Explicitness comes through careful analysis of the language, the rules, the vocabulary, the texts, the skills, the tasks, the spoken and the written features, the relation with content areas, the registers and the rhetoric, the needs and the expectations, the test questions and items. Control of uncertainty comes from careful sampling of items and subjects and appropriate matching of them both, from care and skill with item writing, from sensible use and understanding of appropriate statistical procedures and from a general sense of confidence in uncertainty itself. Item analysis and descriptive statistics are indeed means to this end so that we know what it is − and how inadequately − we are claiming; and at the same time that we appreciate that the claim has been made stronger by the refining use of those very statistical procedures.

Two other terms for what we have called making explicit and controlling uncertainty are *validity* and *reliability*. It is not surprising therefore that the argument of this book, its continuing theme, is the reactive relation between managing explicitness and controlling uncertainty because that is equivalent to saying that the book is about validity and reliability, the chief themes of any testing discussion. We will return to explicitness (validity) and controlling uncertainty (reliability) later, but we also constantly refer to them throughout the book.

Concerns of Linguistics

Linguistics may be defined in a narrow or in a broad sense. In the narrow sense linguistics studies language as a system (or set of systems) in its own right in order to establish language rules, this is the internal or microlinguistic approach. In the broad sense linguistics studies language as a form of behaviour, in relation to other behaviours in the individual and in society in order both to help establish rules for those other behaviours and to illuminate language uses and language roles. We are concerned here with the narrower sense of linguistics, the broader aspects will be taken up later.

The narrower sense of linguistics includes both theoretical and descriptive concerns: *theoretical* because linguistics is said to be the scientific study of language and all scientific disciplines involve theory, and *descriptive* as the necessary other aspect of scientific study, both for its own sake so as to catalogue the languages of the world and − from the point of view of (narrower) linguistics more importantly − in order to test or validate the theory/theories. In other words, the better the theory the more universal it is, the more readily it allows for descriptions of yet more languages, especially those from different language families. A linguistic theory remains a hypothesis as long as its descriptive apparatus can be applied only to one language: the more languages it entertains the more powerful − as theory − it becomes.

Linguistic theories commonly face *three major problems*: first their universality, second their combining power and third their incorporation of extra language data. We will now look at each of these in turn and then consider them in relation to language testing.

Problems of Linguistic Theories

Universality

A view of language as an interlocking system of systems is straightforward enough for it to apply across languages. It would be unthinkable in any linguistic theory for a natural language not to have a sound system (and therefore a level of phonology), a meaning system (and therefore a semantic level), and a combining system (a level of syntax). Theories may differ as to how these relate and whether to admit other systems as systems (for example a pragmatic level, a discourse level, a context level), but there is really no dispute about the need to posit three main systems. Similarly with high-level sentence rules. All linguistic theories accept that their purpose is to provide rules for sentences, the rules are productive or sentence generators. But all that that says is that the highest linguistic unit is the sentence (putting aside the contentious issue of whether higher linguistic units than the sentence can be specified), or, to put it another way, that linguistics is about sentence structure. So far so good: just as all languages have a phonology, a grammar and a semantics so all languages have sentences.

For a linguistic theory to be of any interest, however, it must provide more information, such as that a sentence is made up of parts, themselves made up of further parts, combining and recombining in various ways. No doubt linguistic theories may again agree that sentences contain subjects and predicates, that is that there is an X about which some statement is made (or predicated).

However, problems arise, even at this still high level of generality, as to whether the focus of the sentence is on subject or on predicate, and so on. Undoubtedly there is universality across languages just as there is a common humanity across peoples, but what is universal is either a set of components (the categories or parts of speech of a traditional grammar) or a very small set of phrase structure (or structural) rules which will indicate that all languages possess and combine in similar ways subjects and predicates, subjects and objects, nouns and verbs. Thereafter theories have to resort to some form of controlled ad hoc rearrangements or transformations. So again at a very high level of generality it can be said that all languages can be analysed linguistically into rules and exceptions. The aim of all theories is to increase the rules and limit the exceptions.

Combining power

The problem of combination has already been addressed. If it is a problem for generalizing across languages, it is equally an intra-language problem between systems (how, say, grammar and semantics combine), between systems and part systems (how, for example, semantics and discourse combine), and within systems (how parts of the grammar combine so as to produce and generate sentences, and how discourse, for example, can be reduced to rule). This is of course the fundamental task of linguistic theories and inevitably they cope as has already been suggested by various solutions of rule plus exceptions (or transformations).

'All grammars leak' is a way of accepting two things: first, the interperson variation such that at a certain point a separate grammar is needed for each individual speaker, as evidenced by the well-known fact of native-speaker disagreement; and second, the accounting for what a single native speaker can do, that is to say that a grammar can only go so far as a linguistic description even though it must be the case that native speakers control or know a much more elaborate grammar than can be described. This is only another way of saying that for the native speaker those no man's land areas of discourse and intonation are indeed rule-governed, but what those rules are, and how they combine with grammar, phonology and semantics, it is difficult to say. Hence, of course, the attempt through more refined theory to incorporate more and more in the description.

Incorporation of extra-linguistic data

The problems noted above have to do with language as a form of independent behaviour, treating it as if it took place in a laboratory, in isolation from other behaviours and forms of organization. But language is never, except in linguistic descriptions, an independent activity; it always takes place in social and historical settings, it is always produced by and indicative of individual processes, it always refers backwards and forwards in time, thus demanding that previous knowledge and indeed world knowledge be drawn on and shared. Reducing such knowledge to rule is problematic. Most linguists consider that a linguistic theory should be conservative, relying for its clarity on those areas that can be defined and leaving the rest to psychologists, sociologists, political scientists, stylisticians and ethnomethodologists. This may be satisfactory for a linguistic *theory* but it will hardly do for linguistic *applications*.

Attention to extra-linguistic data, as long as the data are regarded as *extra*, outside, moves linguistics from its narrow or micro-focus to its broad or macro-focus, from the linguistics of language systems to the bracketed linguistics (sociolinguistics, psycholinguistics, ethnolinguistics, computational linguistics and so on). If, on the other hand, the data are regarded as being potentially inside, that is as colonizable by linguistics, then of course linguistic systems expand themselves or multiply into more systems in order to incorporate the claimed data. Such an approach might claim that linguistics must of necessity explain or account for cognitive processes, language acquisition, contextual settings, or language variety. These claims are commonly made by psycholinguists and sociolinguists on behalf of the data at the centre of their attention, which they regard as rule-governed and which they claim are part of language. It will be noted that the narrow and the broad approaches are equivalent to the areas of explicitness and uncertainty. Indeed, the rival claims of the two can be found within the narrow approach alone, since theories however narrow acquire uncertainty as they seek explicitness about the extra data they are incorporating; or, to express the equation more graphically:

Explicitness + data = uncertainty; or E + D = U.

The very act of incorporation, of constructing theories and writing grammars (although these are necessary and welcome acts), leads to uncertainty, but an uncertainty that must be admitted and accepted. We now turn to the relation of language testing to these three problem areas.

The Linguistic Problem Areas and Language Testing

Universals and language testing

This is the least serious of the problem areas for language testing since tests are by their nature tests of particular languages. However, in the areas of language aptitude, language acquisition and bilingualism, comparability of tests across languages would be of value: language aptitude because of the desirability of being able to make general statements, in the sense that language aptitude is of interest only if it is generalizable. Similarly with language acquisition, where again both the linguistic and the learning interest are in the general processes and properties of acquisition rather than in the acquisition of one language. That being so, both child-language acquisition and second-language acquisition studies can only benefit from comparable methodologies and procedures, and categories of a hypothesized natural order, that is from more powerful as well as more detailed linguistic theories.

Bilingual studies can also benefit from more universal linguistic theories since statements about bilingualism (both in terms of balance in individual bilingualism and in terms of societal bilingualism in such studies as mutual intelligibility) would be more valid were there matching or comparability across the languages in question.

Combining power and language testing

It is here that the normative nature of language testing becomes evident. As we have seen, language varies between individuals (hence the problem for a language description which is more than very high-level abstraction). It also varies within one individual, in the sense that ontogenetic development is life-long. Hence the problem of writing a grammar for even one individual. Language tests have so far done no better than linguistic grammars, proposing an idealized form of the language for the test. What is likely is that a test will favour a particular subgroup in society, often a more advantaged group with higher socio-economic status. Individual members of such a subgroup will vary linguistically but it remains the case that they are more like one another than they are like less advantaged groups. The choice of such a subgroup as the model or target or norm of the test is made inevitable by the proximity of the educational model to this subgroup's variety, the elaborated code of Bernstein (1971), and the educated standard of the written language, which cannot but have a washback effect on the forms of speech of those who traditionally succeed most in education, that is this same subgroup.

The effect is to exaggerate and perhaps increase the already existing social disadvantage of those whose language variety is different. This is, of course, only an extreme case of a societal situation in which the privileged minority's language is the language of education, thereby decreasing the access and the likely success of the underprivileged majority. No doubt it would be desirable for language tests to incorporate variation just as it is desirable for grammars to do so. The sociolinguistic extension of the latter is one way of admitting and providing for language variation within grammars. The proposed employment within testing of second-language acquisition elicitation techniques for scoring and analysis indicate how tests may eventually be able to incorporate language variation also (Pienemann and Johnson 1984). However, it must be asked to what extent such admission of variation into tests is desirable even if it is possible, given that not only do tests now clearly operate as norms but that perhaps that is what they must do and, indeed, what they do best. As soon as we accept that a test or an examination is a measure of language behaviour we have to agree that it must be normative since measures are not case-histories but methods of comparison. Thus tests can only be norms; but that is what we want them to be, since the purpose of testing is to provide relative information.

There is a further problem for language testing in relation to the combining power of language systems and to the linguistic failure to comprehend that power. Language tests are capable of handling language elements. Testing for control of elements in the grammar or other linguistic systems is after all the well-tried discrete point method of testing. However, the very nature of language systems is that they combine (indeed as we have seen it is to some extent an artefact of the linguistic analysis that presents linguistic systems as separate), that the grammar and the semantics interlock. We are, of course, still not discussing the ways in which those systems are used; an analogy might be the medical analysis of the body into systems (coronary, urinary, etc.), and then the synthesis into a system of systems, that is the human body which is still only a plan, a blueprint, and not an account of what happens or indeed what can happen to an individual body/person. Similarly, language systems combine together as the overall language system: we will return later to the important distinctions between, first, the language system and the account of what can be done with the system and, second, between what can be done and what actually is done with the language system.

It may be argued that a test of the overall language 'system' (notice we are not saying of all *skills* but of the overall *system*) is in fact no more than a set of tests of the systems − much as a complete physical examination will test all the body's component systems in order to arrive at a judgement about an overall physical state. In essence this is an argument about the factorial structure of language proficiency and we will take this up more fully later in the chapter.

Meanwhile it does indeed remain the case that linguistic descriptions do not provide any compellingly satisfactory account of system combination, and therefore what passes for a test of the overall language system is either a disguised grammar test or a confusing mixture, a kind of shotgun approach to combination in which cloze and dictation are recent favoured examples, with the framework essay and the structured interview older favourites. The point is that there is no way of designing a language test to test the *language* system (as there certainly is to test *linguistic* systems) because there exists no rationale to tell us how linguistic systems combine. All we can do is guess, recognizing that any language sample must provide features of all linguistic systems and that syntax is likely to dominate in any sample we choose. By saying this, we admit what cloze and dictation results typically show, namely, that what cloze, dictation and similar compromise instruments test is principally grammar.

Incorporation of extra-linguistic data and language testing

The tension between explicitness and uncertainty is, it has been argued, endemic to all linguistic enterprise: but it becomes most strained here in the attempts to incorporate within linguistic systematic description the stuff of language use, those marginal areas where system is uncertain, in which language interacts with social and psychological systems, above all to provide determinacy for contextual language use. If we consider this well-known example from Sapir (1921):

the farmer killed the duckling

the grammar and the semantics (and the phonology when spoken) of the sentence are straightforward. What is problematic is what are the dynamics of such a sentence: which farmer, why did he kill the duckling, where, who said so, what elicited this statement anyway, to which question or first statement could this sentence act as a response, what could be the next statement, would such a statement be equally likely from young and old, male and female, is it a standard form, does it suggest casual or formal style and so on. Why should anyone say this, is it a comment, a description, or a criticism? All such questions concern the status of this sentence in contextual settings: the aim of the additive linguistic disciplines is to incorporate such concerns within linguistic systematization.

The area of most difficulty for language testing (apart, as we have seen, from the special case of language aptitude testing) is in the attempt to develop true performance tests, a good example of which is communicative language testing. The impetus to develop communicative language tests comes from the communicative language teaching movement, itself a response on the pedagogical side to the continuing inadequacy of more traditional structural methods and to a general move in pedagogy (and therefore in language teaching) from a deductive to an inductive philosophy, and, on the linguistic side, primarily from the extension of linguistics into social context or the attempted incorporation of sociolinguistic data of which we have spoken.

This is a powerful double-edged tool and communicative language teaching has had an important influence on language teaching *developments* and *thinking*, though it is not clear how much it has actually influenced *practice*. The problems that arise for language testing are precisely that language testing needs to be clear, in this case explicit, about what is under test. Paradoxically, as we have noted above, there is no such constraint on communicative language *teaching*, since the teacher can explain and expand what the tasks, the exercises, the lessons only hint at by making them come alive and so have immediate communicative effect, in other words, tolerate the central uncertainty of such tasks and not demand explicitness.

That is precisely what tests, as tests, must do. In testing this is desirable both for the language input, that is the construction of tasks, and for the measurement output. Some flexibility is possible between the input and the output, more uncertainty on the input side (for example, vagueness as to the *language* content of the tasks) is acceptable but only if it is accompanied by greater certainty on the output side (firming up the scales or grids for scoring). This has traditionally been the case for tests of both spoken and written production where care has been taken to objectify the open-ended tasks of essay-writing and interviews (open-ended even when they are constrained by frameworks and skeletons).

To return to our Sapir example:

the farmer killed the duckling

A really strict grammar question would focus on morphology and in fact on the testee's knowledge of grammar, thus:

Put the correct past tense marker:
The farmer killed the duckling

A less strict item might concentrate on sequence, thus:

Put these words in a correct sequence:
farmer, duckling, killed, the, the

Already, it will be observed, the strict grammar constraint has been relaxed since the 'correct' response must be:

the farmer killed the duckling

and not

the duckling killed the farmer

since both are grammatically well formed on the information given. Let us now add a time marker so as to facilitate testing for tense, thus:

Which of these is correct?
a.   Yesterday, the farmer kills the duckling

b. Yesterday the farmer killing the duckling
c. Yesterday the farmer killed the duckling
d. Yesterday the farmer will kill the duckling

The 'correct' response is, of course, (c) − but the assumption has been made in the item construction that the testee will be aware of the time−tense relationship. Already then the discreteness of the linguistic system has had to be broken down and indeed this is the case for much, perhaps most, discrete testing in the structural tradition except perhaps for very discrete phonemic tests. Of course it is legitimate to maintain that grammatical control of, for example, the English past tense assumes an awareness of the tense−time relationship. However, even in this very narrow example the explicitness of what is being tested has already shifted into slight (if in this case trivial) uncertainty. How much more uncertainty must a performance test accept!

So let us go back to the farmer and the duckling, this time regarding it as a potential utterance in a real context of situation and not just as an exemplar sentence of English. Let us then regard the sentence:

the farmer killed the duckling

as a possible response or as the second member of a two-part response pair. What is of interest is what the first part could be, thus:

Which of the following sentences (a, b, c) is most likely to elicit the response
the farmer killed the duckling?
a. Who killed the duckling?
b. What did the farmer do to the duckling?
c. What did the farmer kill?

In fact all three questions are possible first-part members. No doubt the canonical choice is (c), given that in unmarked theme the new information comes at the end of the response and since **farmer** and **killed** are given in (c) then the new information must be **duckling**. But there is no reason to exclude (a) and (b) since we cannot assume that theme is unmarked nor can we presume to judge how the sentence:

the farmer killed the duckling

is read, that is any one of the content words may receive the main information tonic. One solution would be to accept all three choices as 'correct' but inevitably that would imply giving the benefit of the doubt to the testee that he or she is both aware that all three choices are all possible and also under what circumstances. The limiting case would be if a testee were to select (a). Should that be regarded as *incorrect*? In a structural type test it would be but it can hardly be wrong in a communicative test. It is of course the case that once we admit into the equation the testee's awareness of context *everything* becomes possible. It is a common experience of language test construction that native speakers used in piloting tests for learners will claim that for them 'incorrect' choices are correct. They are of course relying on their contextual intuitions.

What this discussion has been intended to demonstrate is that in language testing as in linguistics the incorporation of more data, in this case context, loses explicitness as it gains uncertainty, or:

$$E + D = U.$$

Testing Languages for Specific Purposes (LSP)

The two problems of combining power and of incorporating extra language data come together (as we shall see in chapter 6) in the field of Languages for Specific Purposes (LSP). Here we are concerned with the interlocking of linguistic systems, with variation (register differences) and with the relation of language system to the social context in terms of institutional differences between, for example, science and journalism or between different kinds of science or between different genres of text types (such as narrative and expository). LSP is pedagogically important because it enables the learner to avoid the general in favour of the particular, reminding us of Blake's line: 'Virtue resides in minute particulars'. At least it is on those grounds that it has gained support − the pedagogic problem of course is whether the general and the particular/specific are so different that it is useful to teach them separately. Equally problematic is the extension of this question into whether or not the specific purposes are different, and how far they are different, from one another. LSP has further pedagogic importance because it has been used to argue for a delay in beginning language teaching until adulthood and to justify language teaching without literature. It can be argued that all language teaching is a form of LSP, even so-called general language, general English or whatever. But in fact this begs the really interesting question which is not pedagogical but linguistic: to what extent one LSP differs linguistically from another and to what extent there is a *linguistic* common core, to what extent the LSP is *content* and not just *face* validity. This is not to say of course that there is no serious pedagogical issue involved. Even if it could be demonstrated that linguistically there is no reason to separate, say, scientific English from non-scientific English, it could still be important both for motivational and for familiarity reasons to use an LSP approach. Face validity has its uses and its arguments too.

We will consider LSP from the point of view of English (thus ESP), since there seems no reason to believe that English is at all special in this regard: the fact that English may be at the moment the favoured international language of science is for the purposes of this argument irrelevant.

There are two apparently but not substantially contradictory arguments against LSP on linguistic grounds. The first argument is how, on what principled linguistic grounds, can one variety be distinguished from another; the second is how, once the process has started it can be stopped. It will be observed that these two arguments are exactly those found in the language— dialect distinction and attempts to distinguish on linguistic grounds between language and dialect are unsuccessful: indeed it is not easy to distinguish linguistically between languages, given the political nature of language definition.

On what linguistic grounds then can scientific English be distinguished from, let us say, journalistic English? The usual answer is that there are no linguistic grounds on which such a distinction can be made, that in terms of linguistic systems there is no principled way in which such a distinction could be made. There are however two possible ways in which such a distinction may be contemplated: *first*, that there is differential *use* of linguistic systems (for example more passives, fewer transitions, more definite articles), and *second*, that there may be systematic distinctions within those marginal systems we have spoken of, discourse, pragmatics. In addition, of course, there will necessarily be important differences in lexical choices and these will have some influence on differential semantic use. Furthermore, differential lexical uses are very important from a pedagogical viewpoint since knowledge of specific content words may both assist and prevent understanding. So we can agree that major language varieties such as scientific English and journalistic English may be distinguishable in terms of lexical choice, grammar and semantic use, and, less certainly, discourse and pragmatic systems. But we really must be clear as to what can be claimed in terms of such systematic difference, as will be seen when we look at the issue in reverse. So far we have asked the question whether or not such distinctions can be made at all and we have decided that yes, they may be in terms of use. We are less clear about distinctions in terms of system.

The second argument continues the question: can such distinctions be brought to a halt or, once started, is there a principled reason for refusing to make further distinctions among specific purposes? Having distinguished scientific from journalistic English can we now distinguish among varieties of scientific English, both in terms of content or subject matter (for example, physics, medicine, astronomy, etc.) and in terms of style or methodology? That is to say: are some scientific Englishes more formal than others, more spoken, more laboratory reporting, more research-oriented, can the research reports be distinguished in terms of subject or specific purpose? In all these cases the question we return to is *in terms of what?* Indeed it may be the case that the English of X uses more spoken English than the English of Y, but that is a feature of language use not of linguistic difference. And so on for the other uses. The issue comes back always to the theoretical one of discrete linguistic varieties and it looks again as though, once we have admitted a difference in terms of use between science and non-science, there is no legitimate reason for refusing to accept further distinctions *ad infinitum* until of course, logically, we arrive at individual use (and that too we have seen is not completely systematic).

The most sensible position seems to be that there are indeed differences between major language uses, themselves defined on institutional grounds, for example scientific and political, that these differences have language use correlates, that to some extent these are systematic, that this is a very important pedagogical question and that it is no more (or less) possible to pin down these systematic variations than anywhere else in linguistic descriptions, and that basically we should treat it as a pragmatic issue, and not a theoretical one.

The implications for testing are therefore very clear. Tests of LSP/ESP are indeed possible but they are distinguished from one another on non-theoretical terms. Their variation depends on practical and ad hoc distinctions which cannot be substantiated. In other words, such tests should be determined on entirely pragmatic grounds such that their separate status relates to occasions which are quite non-linguistic, for example the existence of institutional support such as separate teaching provision or professional divisions (as in doctor/dentist, chemist/biochemist). In all such cases it is necessary to re-member that there is a pragmatic imperative and a testing imperative, in addition to a linguistic argument.

Let me add a footnote here. The LSP/ESP approach provides us with a paradox, namely that the desire to provide for variety through delineating the specific purposes may lead to the strait-jacket of exact specification. Tests such as those suggested by, for example, B.J. Carroll (1980) are still at the programmatic level and it remains to be seen how different they will actually be. This, after all, is the real issue over the testing of communicative perform-ance. Is the teaching (and therefore the testing) of communicative competence best seen as a *syllabus* issue or as a *method* issue? Often it seems to be more about strategy than about basic content. If it is about strategy, then the case for replacing linguistic tests by communicative ones disappears and communi-cative tests (and teaching) appear as another version of linguistic tests. If there is a real difference then we may query whether non-native-speaking language teachers can use a communicative syllabus if they cannot in fact turn a structural syllabus to communicative ends. What remains a convincing argument in favour of linguistic competence tests (both discrete point and integrative) is that grammar is at the core of language learning. Grammar is far more powerful in terms of generalizability than any other language feature. Therefore grammar may still be the most salient feature to teach, and to test.

Psycholinguistics and Second-Language Acquisition

Psycholinguistics extends linguistics into traditional psychological concerns. Linguistics is now once again reduced to its micro-formulation, to the narrow sense of the three major linguistic systems, of phonology, grammar, semantics. These, it will now be clear, concern an idealized state of language in that they are concerned with the systems of language structure and not with the use of that system. They are, in Saussure's terms, concerned with *langue* or in

Chomsky's, with *competence*. What psycholinguistics is about is not that form of idealization but the operationalizing in the individual of that *langue/*competence, along with the deregularizing of the ideal and with the analysis of the channel, medium and brain constraints both in and through time on that competence. It has been helpfully suggested that the business of psycholinguistics is with the description and analysis of performance, taking competence for granted. Note that performance in this sense does not mean language use, but rather the mechanisms of language use, an idealization in itself as complete as the linguistic idealization of competence. Psycholinguistic interests in language processing, in language capacity, in language and cognition and in language acquisition (focusing on the mother tongue, less on a second language) are of relevance to language testing.

One important area (perhaps the most important) of applied linguistics, broadly interpreted, which has come into prominence in the last 10−15 years is that of second-language acquisition research. There are good reasons for the emergence of this field into so central a position: second-language acquisition brings together a theoretical interest in the nature of language acquisition (and therefore in the important linguistic issues of universal grammar and of linguistic competence) with a practical concern for teaching and learning second languages. Furthermore, second-language acquisition (SLA) provides for linguistics and psycholinguistics a special case of language acquisition which may well be crucial in consideration of the nature of language, given that the target language second-language acquirer has already acquired the first language and it is therefore possible to relate the second and the first and to view the second as a pure example of linguistic acquisition, unlike the first which is inevitably bound up with the whole process of child development and cognitive growth.

In addition, SLA research has brought together a specific theory with a viable methodology, interlanguage, the developmental model of successive approximations through states of interlanguage towards the target language. It also provides a changing methodology moving from the negative method of error analysis to the more positive morpheme studies, communication strategies and, most recently, a combination of data types indicative of what the learner can do rather than can't do (for example with judgements). This has not dispensed with error analysis as a tool and it is customary now to use both test and spontaneous production data as additive information on the learner's language state. What such a methodology attempts to capture is the process of learning rather than only the product. More sophisticated statistical analysis such as implicational scaling (deriving from Guttman and Thurstone scales used for questionnaire and survey data) have assisted this move from negative error counts to positive feature successes. It would be unjust, however, to claim that error analysis was always and only negative. It was not, certainly not on purpose. The purpose of error analysis was always to indicate how much the learner knew rather than how much he or she did not know. Again, such a method was inevitably concerned with process, if one accepts that process involves a series of small-scale products.

One interesting point of contact with testing for SLA research is found in judgements and appropriacy testing. Such tests are concerned, however, with establishing rather than setting a measure: as such, they are more like tests in production than tests in use, since their purpose is to examine the agreement and the variation among learners, and the extent to which such variation relates to other variables such as levels of proficiency, age, first language, or type of input received. Such judgement tests are not concerned with rank order or with criterion referencing. No doubt it would be possible to use such tests at a later date as a second stage as 'tests' but it is difficult to know for what purpose.

However, the sensible approach may be less dogmatic and restrictive, perhaps by accepting that testing is itself both a *product* (for example, a language proficiency test, an aptitude test) and a *method* (for example, judgement tests in second-language acquisition research). The outcome in both cases is much the same: the distinction is that language tests are ends in themselves, they are not intended to provide explanation-seeking information in other research areas, but what they do provide is firm, reliable evidence on levels of norm-referenced proficiency. They publish norms which allow learners to be located in terms of learner populations. Second-language acquisition research testing, on the other hand, is for something else (in this case, second-language acquisition research): no norms are provided, the purpose is explanatory and fact-finding.

So much then for the use of testing in second-language acquisition research, but what of the reverse, in the more general sense? What influence does second-language acquisition (or psycholinguistic theory generally) have on language testing? The evidence here is slight and what there is suggests that there is very little influence. Language testing in terms of methodology is still firmly committed to an error analysis type of approach in which rights and wrongs are totalled and scores attributed. True, other methods of data collection (in terms of what the learner knows) are attempted. Such methods are concerned particularly with production performance and involve judgements of that performance, spoken and written, but in so doing, testing is even less easily qualitative than second-language acquisition research in relation to data from spontaneous production. In terms of language model, psycholinguistics has been a little more influential in that it can perhaps be claimed that just as sociolinguistics has influenced language testing with its emphasis on communication (hence attempts at tests of communicative competence), so psycholinguistics has contributed to the concepts of processing of information and of redundancy, thereby legitimizing such testing techniques as cloze and dictation.

Redundancy of tests, indeed of speech/language in general is what makes prediction possible. No doubt a non-predictable language is in principle thinkable but in practice it couldn't operate as a human language since its processing demands would be too onerous, each unit (not only word but morpheme, phoneme) would require an equal amount of interpretative processing. The effect would be short or very restrictive messages, because, of course, language is redundant at all levels. It would mean that even the most frequent ritualistic phrases such as greetings would have to be processed on each utterance occasion as if new because there would be no tacit understanding of situation or of language. Language fluency would be equivalent to language learning and there would be no native speakers. All language use would be like aphasics recovering but never succeeding. Clearly this cannot represent language or language use as we know it. *Equally clearly, if redundancy and its concomitant, fluency of prediction, is so crucial then it should be central to all language testing.*

We have mentioned the specific techniques of cloze (and its variants) and dictation but all tests of the spoken language necessarily involve a high degree of prediction, with in this case the practical issue of repetition of the text stimulus, in that successive repetition necessarily lowers the demand on prediction. Study skills tests of reading put a high premium on prediction but of course all reading demands prediction of a discourse type. Indeed, writing tests necessarily demand a control over those basic discourse features of cohesion and coherence, indicating that the testee can write acceptably, with normal fluent built-in reader prediction. The more discourse-like the text and/or task provided the greater the demand on prediction, but all tests require normal predictive ability given the centrality of this ability to language use.

Psycholinguistics then is of major importance in language testing – and that should not surprise us. Language tests are attempts to encapsulate language knowledge and they can succeed in this only if they focus on the main characteristics of language and of language ability: this is another way of saying that linguistics, both micro- and macro-, is of importance in language testing.

Factorial Study of Language Proficiency

One area of psycholinguistic relevance in language testing research is that of the *factorial structure* of abilities (see chapter 6). This is, in psychology and education, an old song, of importance in all ability constructs in terms of psychological theory and ability testing. It has had a particular importance in research into general and specific abilities (for example, intelligence testing) and therefore has considerable relevance to applications in selection, education and vocational guidance. It is also relevant to curriculum planning and choice in schools where the issue of range of subjects offered relates to the amount of differential variance shared by different subject areas.

Now if the discussion about intelligence is at all sensible, that is, if there really is any reality in the concept of general intelligence, then it would seem supererogatory to question general language ability. But that is the issue which has taken up attention and it has, of course, an important practical outcome. The theoretical aspect we can assume, but it is of importance practically in, for example, selection of a minimum set of language tests for a proficiency battery, or in drawing up a plan for a language aptitude test. What remains very problematical, however, is whether the means at our disposal for research are any better than the practical instruments we have available, that is whether it really is any more than a practical issue. Much of the argument and debate has been over statistical procedures and interpretations and only slightly less over experimental design.

The question that has been addressed is whether language ability can be explained in terms of one general ability which underlies all language knowledge and use or in terms of two or more abilities (such as production and comprehension, spoken and written). Now there appear to be two ways of dealing with this question apart from continued research activity which so far has led only to quite opposing outcomes and explanations. The two solutions are: *first*, that there is no possibility of a unique explanation since the type of outcome reached depends entirely on the method of analysis used. And factor analysis is in principle not one but (at least) two main method types, that of factor analysis (proper) and principal components analysis. One method logically derives one main factor and then a series of secondary factors; the other proceeds immediately to the derivation of a binary (or multiple) factor structure.

Each method, as is obvious, is predicated on a particular type of psychological view of human abilities: neither is 'right', both use a model of ability which they impose on the data under analysis. In other words, language ability (like 'intelligence') is both unifactorial and multifactorial. So that way only frustration and chaos lie if the method of factor analysis is being used (as alas! it has been) as a discovery procedure rather than as is appropriate as a way of rearranging data for model fit, that is as confirmatory factor analysis.

The *second* solution is to recognize that the primary question necessarily has different answers depending on the level of abstraction at which it is asked (and which is expected in the answer). At the more abstract level the answer can only be that there is one general ability (of which language ability is one component). At a less abstract level we note that there is a separate and independent language ability, and at a less abstract level still we further note that there are several language abilities, not one. Such solutions do not solve the initial research question since they do not tell us what is the 'true' state of language abilities, whether one or more. But instead they liberate us from the need to find a solution to what is basically an uninteresting, indeed a non-theoretical question. They help us realize that the question does not need an answer, is not indeed a real question, and that the issue is much more a practical than a theoretical one. The way we resolve it depends on either what we must do in a local situation of practical test need or what sort of question we think we are asking.

Let us look at the testing implications in more detail. We take two instances in order to examine two uses of factor analysis. First a proficiency battery for preliminary filtering of large numbers of secondary-school students seeking admission to a restricted number of places in an English medium university. Here we turn to factor analysis for its efficiency and treatment of redundancy and efficiency. We want as short a battery as possible, which will do the job for us in terms of prediction and regression combinations. This is essentially a very practical use of factor analysis. One method of factor analysis would show that some selection of parts of all sub-tests would indicate proficiency best, but the other method would show that perhaps two of the sub-tests would achieve the same level of prediction. We use factor analysis here to reduce the battery if possible because it will tell us if there is overlap of test instruments. It is of course true that the same information is already available for us in the correlation matrix. Factor analysis will not tell us more than a careful interpretation of a set of correlations will, but factor analysis does go further in that it looks at interaction among a set of tests and not only at the relationship between individual tests or sub-tests.

In this chapter an attempt has been made to show that language testing must compromise between uncertainty and explicitness and not attempt to exaggerate one at the expense of the other. In chapter 6 we argue firmly for the central role of language testing in applied linguistics. Our view is that it is through its important contribution to the fundamental linguistic tension between uncertainty and explicitness that the central role of language testing in applied linguistics can be generally agreed.

6 Language Testing and Applied Linguistics

The Development of Applied Linguistics

The argument in chapters 1–5 has been that language testing provides the best estimate we have of the aims of our language learning, of how to realize and describe those goals and of how to assess the extent to which they have been reached. We have located this defining role of language testing at the centre of applied linguistics and we now turn directly to consider that relationship.

Chapter 6 also acts as a bridge between the discussion of language tests as measures of learners and their learning to their parallel use as a methodology for evaluating language teaching projects. In point of fact, we shall in chapters 7–9 interpret *project* very broadly so as to include 'reflexive' projects which are themselves about test development as well as the more obvious curriculum, learning and teaching projects. Our argument will continue to be that language tests used in evaluation, just as much as those used in more straightforward testing, must still reconcile the twin demands of validity and reliability or, in the other terms we have used, of uncertainty and explicitness.

Applied linguistics has in the last twenty years developed as a coherent discipline by identifying those areas of linguistics, sociolinguistics, psychology of language and education, which inform our understanding of the processes of language learning, notably in institutional settings, with particular reference to language teaching. In so doing it has gone from fragmented attempts to provide a framework for rational discussions of language teaching to a more theoretical approach to language teaching and to language use. So far the greatest effort in applied linguistics has been in relation to language teaching and, to a lesser extent, language pathologies, but the way is now open for a more dynamic approach which will inform, and in due course explain, other aspects of language use.

As part of the development over these two decades, the discipline of applied linguistics has properly and necessarily formulated its own experimental procedures which permit the testing of hypotheses drawn from the theoretical statements and which provide descriptive apparatuses for an examination in terms of analyses of the linguistic data which the theories demand. The three main sources for the experimental and descriptive developments have been:

1 language testing,
2 second-language acquisition studies, and
3 discourse analysis.

Of these the most applied is language testing in that it so obviously recognizes its concern with practical issues of language demands and selection requirements. But as Lado's key study (Lado 1961) made clear (and thereby setting the agenda for work on language testing over the following twenty years), language testing provides both practical solutions to language teaching problems and an examination of central applied linguistics concerns: the nature of language proficiency, language aptitude and the delineation of language learning stages.

There is a proper dynamic in the growth of a discipline. As it develops, its parts grow and prosper at different rates and jostle for the high ground. In so doing, their very success can take them away from the centre of the discipline which they inform to a potentially separate existence, thus creating, or threatening to create, a new discipline.

SLA research (see chapter 5) is a striking example of such a trend. It grew out of the practice of error analysis which was employed as a methodology for contrastive studies, itself an earlier explanatory theory for applied linguistics. SLA research has now become important as a theoretical study in its own right, dislodging contrastive analysis from its explanatory status and becoming itself a mode of description, with its own methodology and analysis. In addition it now has its own set of competing theories, as is the nature of theory development. There is a tendency now for SLA research to regard itself as no longer part of applied linguistics, but as a discrete discipline.

While such a trend is normal as disciplines grow and develop, it is, in fact, unnecessary in terms of the second-language acquisition—applied linguistics relationship. Applied linguistics itself has moved on during the period of SLA research growth to a reorientation of itself as being concerned with language learning, which as a wider and more basic study than language teaching may well become the theoretical and descriptive study of language in use. Applied linguistics needs SLA research as a major set of explanatory and descriptive apparatuses, and SLA research, on the other hand, equally needs applied linguistics to give it context and purpose.

Language testing development over the same period (roughly the last 20 years) represents a parallel dialectic, moving from a peripheral role in applied linguistics at the time of Lado's *Language Tests* (1961) to a commanding position within applied linguistics precisely because it has confronted major questions of language learning and language use by articulating viable methodologies. What language testing has done in the last 20 years has been to move itself from having only a practical to having both a practical and a theoretical status within applied linguistics. As such it has gained academic respect (always given more readily to theoretical studies), and has begun to develop explanatory power. At the same time it has lost some of its practical force and development value in language teaching: while its *theoretical* modelling has developed very fast, its *practical* applications have not kept pace even with developments in language teaching (for example, communicative language teaching).

This may parallel the development over the last 20 years of SLA research with the research element moving forward from contrastive analysis and the practical link to language teaching, powerful (though no doubt theoretically unsound) at the error analysis stage, gradually weakening as the theoretical and research aspect becomes stronger until current second-language acquisition scholars typically claim that their discipline has as much − or as little − concern with language teaching as has, say, theoretical linguistics. And when one such second-language acquisition scholar (e.g. Krashen 1982) makes a direct connection with his Input Hypotheses between language teaching and his acquisition-learning distinction, the insights provided for language teaching are but momentary and the gain in methodology non-existent. It is of particular interest to our present discussion that there are signs in some current thinking about second-language acquisition of there being a need for a rapprochement between second-language acquisition studies and language testing, see for example Pienemann and Johnson (1984), Brindley (1986), Long (1984).

The paradox we face, therefore, is that development in applied linguistics is away from language teaching concerns and interests. At one level this must be inevitable. What starts as a subject (teaching courses for selected groups of students, often vocational students in the case of applied linguistics) typically develops into a discipline, an area institutionally defined by named posts (Professor of . . .), journals, degrees, etc. Eventually the subject-become-discipline acquires a momentum and, hopefully, a coherence of its own. Thus Applied Linguistics loses its original subject-like direct link with language teaching, as well as its minority identification with theoretical linguistics.

As a parenthesis here we can observe that one effect of such development is, apparently, to move the British problem-related version of applied linguistics (that is, what can we use from different disciplines to help solve language teaching problems?) towards the North American linguistic theory-related version (the distinction has been characterized as British *Applied-Linguistics* and American *Linguistics-Applied*). The reason for postulating such a move is that keener and more detailed interest in 'problems' necessarily generates the demand for generalizability through a more theoretical approach. But as we shall see this move is more apparent than real.

Again, it is indeed true that applied linguistics has made serious attempts over the last twenty years to extend its range of relevance beyond language teaching and especially beyond foreign- or second-language teaching with

English as a Foreign (Second) Language as the canonical case into the pathologies (speech production, hearing, sight, etc.), translation and intrepreting, language planning and engineering, lexicography, speech synthesis and computer modelling, literary stylistics and a range of areas of language in/and social life (where the label is often 'Language and . . . .', for example, Language and Medicine, Language and the Law, Language and Religion, the language of propaganda and so on).

While applied linguistics has made inroads in some of these areas (notably the pathologies and lexicography) and while there is ambiguity about the categorization of sociolinguistics, psycholinguistics and so on (and also, as we have seen, second-language acquisition) there is always a special concern for language teaching, if only because applied linguistics, in spite of its discipline growth, is vocationally oriented; and the largest single vocation for which applied linguistics is thought to be relevant is language teaching. But the truth of our paradox does not stand up to scrutiny. For the move in applied linguistics which we have characterized as being towards theory and research has not in reality taken it away, except at a very surface level, from language teaching.

What has happened, as we see it, is that applied linguistics has attempted to explore the underlying structure of language teaching, to consider its aims, demands, procedures, in a more abstract way and to provide explanations for the behaviour of language teaching (and, more generally, to incorporate the other areas of language use which we have cited). As such it does not purport to 'solve' immediate problems of language teaching nor to improve that teaching directly. What it does is to provide a rationale for the activity we know as language teaching, in all of its manifestations. This must have profound implications for the vocational training that applied linguistics sets out to provide and it has been suggested (Davies 1988) that a more appropriate designation for that vocational training would be *education* in applied linguistics rather than *training* in applied linguistics (compare *teacher education* and *teacher training*). The assumption, which we fully accept, is that an education in applied linguistics provides a combination of theoretical understanding and general methodological skills which are of relevance across a very wide range of language teaching (and indeed language use) situations.

The Development of Language Testing

We can document a similar progress in language testing. As with applied linguistics in general, so with language testing in particular: subject matter has become a sub-discipline, with named posts, in research if not in teaching, textbooks, at least one international journal, qualifications (at least one university certificate). The effect of this move from subject to discipline has certainly been greater coherence, but as we have already seen, it also means more research and more theory which do not appear to be of direct relevance to language teachers. Hence the common complaint from language teaching of 'academic' language testing having nothing to say about, for example, communicative language testing. The fact is (see below) that applied linguistics language testing has a great deal to say of relevance to language teaching and indeed to communicative language testing but usually in terms of fundamental issues (see Alderson and Hughes 1981) rather than in terms of communicative language tests for classroom use. In other words, the relevance is indirect.

Language testing has also extended its range of relevance beyond its earlier focus, in two ways: *first*, by developing measures other than quantitative ones (basically a growing realization of the need to value validity more than reliability) so that qualitative measures of judgement including self-judgements and control and observation are included in the tester's repertoire; and, *second*, by extending the scope of testing to encompass evaluation, evaluation of courses, materials, projects, using both quantitative and qualitative measures of plans, processes and input, as well as measurement of learners' output, the traditional testing approach (see chapters 7, 8 and 9).

But as with the general case of applied linguistics, again the paradox is more apparent than real. The research and theoretical development of language testing has led, it is true, to a less direct concern with the writing of language tests and here critics such as Morrow (1979) are correct. But it has also led to a much clearer view both of the nature of language testing, of the ways in which it can be instrumental in applied linguistics research and be itself an area of applied linguistics for research, and also of the role of language testing within applied linguistics. What we see is that Alderson's plea (Alderson 1979) has already been answered and that our own doubts (Davies 1978) about the connection between language testing and applied linguistics, with language testing on the periphery, were always misguided. Language testing was in reality *always* a chief way of applying linguistics, perhaps more so than most other activities in applied linguistics, in that the selection of material for language tests and the statements made in terms of the results achieved were always of linguistic import, making statements about the nature of language and language learning.

Thus the *Issues* volume (Alderson and Hughes 1981) does indeed represent a bringing up to date by making the field more coherent and reporting recent language testing research in applied linguistics, but it also provides a systematization of language testing that could in fact have been made in a speculative manner (i.e. without, as we have said, the recent empirical work) 20 years earlier (e.g. Lado 1961, Harris 1969, Valette 1977), if the climate had been right. In *Issues* (Alderson and Hughes 1981) three main areas are designated and discussed in depth, with published papers used for discussion, followed by discussants' written comments and an account of the seminar discussions that followed the papers plus the discussants' papers. The three areas regarded as of chief relevance to language testing in applied linguistics are:

1 communicative language testing
2 testing language for specific purposes
3 the unitary competence hypothesis.

In all three cases the discussion is theoretical but equally in all three the implications are practical and have (no doubt indirect) relevance to language learning and teaching. Which is another way of saying that nothing is more practical than a good theory. Again, in all three cases, the topics are of central concern within applied linguistics.

The *first* topic, that of Communicative Language Testing, raises the issues of communication, of authenticity, of language-as-sampling and of abstraction in language selection, as well as of direct and indirect tests, and the relationship within linguistics (and language teaching) of structural systems and their realization and uses. All of these are of equal importance in linguistics and eventually in language teaching and it is the role of applied linguistics to tease out and seek to explain those issues which bridge language theory and language use.

The chief role so far for applied linguistics in relation to communicative language testing seems to be that of providing critical theory as in, for example, the analytical framework provided by Canale and Swain (1980) following on the sociolinguistic ideas of Hymes and Gumperz. The upshot to date still seems to be that communicative language testing means *not* communicative-testing-of-language but the testing-of-communicative-language since, as Morrow (1977) has pointed out, what critically defines communicative language testing is the introduction of real language input rather than some new methodology of testing. As a result those few tests of communicative language that have been developed (the Royal Society of Arts 1980, Savignon 1986) focus on one small area where there is reasonable agreement that the input is direct language; to choose a large amount of input would result in contrived or redundant (and therefore untestworthy) data.

The *second* topic, that of Testing Language for Specific Purposes, concerns at one level the very practical need in many situations for assessing learning in languages for specific purposes (LSP) programmes, usually those related to specific academic subjects or to vocational training. At the same time, in order to make sense of the demand for LSP testing the discussion examines the status (and the validity) of needs analysis systems as well as the more fundamental linguistic question of language variety, for LSP teaching assumes that discrete language varieties can be established and described for learners. The role here of language testing research – precisely applied linguistics research in language testing – is both to examine the methodology of such assessment demands and also, and more profoundly, through operationalizing the question, the idea, speculation, theory, and through acting as testable hypotheses, to query the claims and the status of separate language varieties and therefore of the teaching and testing of LSP. (We have referred here to *LSP* but it should be observed that the best known example of LSP is that of English for Specific Purposes – ESP).

The *third* topic, General Language Proficiency, also referred to as the unitary competence hypothesis (UCH), concerns the seemingly least practical of these three main issues in terms of language testing, namely, the nature of linguistic competence whether it is unitary or multiple. At first sight this has little relevance for language teaching and appears to be trying to resolve a theoretical question about linguistic competence through statistical analyses. However, the issue is of central importance in applied linguistics. It demonstrates, by extensive discussion of language testing research experiments, that an elegant research methodology is possible in applied linguistics through language testing. Further, the issue addressed is important to applied linguistic ideas of language learning and of inter-linguistic relationships. As such it is of course also of practical interest by implication in language teaching and in the design and choice of language tests in terms of, for example, whether all skills (production and reception) are equal and how many separate language tests are needed to assess proficiency, that is, the 'one best test' question.

All three of these important issues – Communicative Language Testing, Testing Language (English) for Specific Purposes and General Language Proficiency Testing – remind us that applied linguistics necessarily focuses on matters of central concern to language learning: Communication, with its emphasis on the role of meaning and the importance of purpose in language learning; English for specific purposes and its attempts to operationalize the pragmatic reality of selected language learning; and General language proficiency which seeks evidence for the factorial structure of language learning. These are all central language learning issues and therefore of importance in applied linguistics. All that is remarkable here is that the investigative role being undertaken on behalf of applied linguistics into these three currently central issues of language learning is that of language testing. It is no wonder then that language testing has now come to be regarded as being firmly within the main area of applied linguistics.

The role of language testing in terms of all three issues is twofold: to provide a research methodology and to raise central theoretical (and eventually practical) issues by operationalizing the theories, thereby providing testable hypotheses. What is clearly needed in the further development of language testing in applied linguistics is a closer link in theory and research between language testing concerns and second-language acquisition research. While SLA research is uniquely concerned and equipped to examine language learning processes over time, language testing provides the methodology for and interest in the assessment of product. The two together might – if a union could be made – provide the profounder insights into and explanation of the relation between process and product that we currently lack, again of course providing theoretical results as well as offering practical implications.

Developments in language testing move over time reactively between thesis and counter-thesis, first maximizing validity then maximizing reliability. Rather than expect some kind of synthesis, an unacceptable stasis, it is probably good and inevitable that development should take this reactive path, given the tension that necessarily exists between reliability and validity. The movement into communicative language testing or, as Oller (1979) would have it, more performance-based tests, has been slow and painful for the reasons already addressed. Clearly such a move is on the side of validity, to move the typically reliable, structuralist, objective, discrete point tests of the 1960s into a more communicative mode. That attempt has been most successful in achievement testing, less so in proficiency testing and not at all in aptitude testing. And before it has run its full course we can already observe a counter movement back to an emphasis on reliability. We will examine these two stages of recent development.

Validity

The move to validity in achievement or attainment testing, which is normally school-based and typically provides control over previous learning, is found in the important work of the Council of Europe resulting in the Unit Credit Scheme (van Ek 1980). This scheme attempts to provide a uniform set of levels of attainment for learners of English throughout Council of Europe member countries (except of course for English first-language countries themselves), and by so doing implicitly − and later explicitly − to test attainment of those stages. In the UK the schemes have been redesigned on a very similar mode for use with the teaching (and testing) of French, German, Italian and Spanish and it is reckoned (Clark 1987) that similar schemes could operate well in any language teaching situation where the language is, generally speaking, used only in the foreign-language classroom.

The motivation for the Council of Europe Unit Credit Scheme has been twofold (although it could be argued that the two aims are two ways of saying the same thing): *first*, to provide a framework of equivalence for all Council of Europe member countries and to do this by providing an equivalence-based set of stages with successive attainment of stages tested by appropriate tests. The *second* motivation has been to make learning communicative through those stages, which has been partly a response to, and partly a struggle to keep ahead of, the public's assumption that communicative teaching and testing have become the norm. They have not; such a public assumption is wrong. Much so-called communicative testing is so only in name, or lays too heavy a burden on the test administrator. We need to ask why there is so little success so far in terms of the proliferation of communicative language tests. Is it because of their deliberate non-use or because of the difficulty in their construction?

In my view it is largely for the second reason, as well as a stubbornly held view among those responsible for testing that language tests are universally applicable and that therefore the most efficient tests are likely to be indirect ones since indirect tests are generalizable because they are removed from local contextual constraints. So it is for reasons partly of belief and partly of efficiency that indirect tests continue to be used so widely, for example, grammar tests as surrogate communicative tests. It would be instructive to be able to argue from data, and Savignon (1986) has tried to provide some, but in the main the argument in this area is based on wont, custom and belief.

As a result such tests are not given much exposure and, more importantly, they are not widely available apart from the Unit Credit Scheme. Central to the Unit Credit Scheme philosophy is the view that teachers should be responsible for their own materials including tests. The Council of Europe scheme is basically criterion-referenced and as such the stages of attainment can be made good sense of by the learner without necessarily becoming wholly routinized. However, it is agreed that materials of the Unit Credit Scheme variety do lean heavily towards interaction routines and the danger exists for teaching as well as for testing of tasks and projects and activities which are so heavily routinized as to become learned by rote, particularly when being used by teachers whose own target language proficiency is low. Such teachers, as we have seen, are likely to seek security in well-rehearsed routines, thereby losing the basic spontaneity of a communicative interaction and even reducing the range afforded by a traditionally structural input. Nevertheless, testing derived from the Unit Credit Scheme is psycholinguistically well-founded in terms of stages of language learning. It appears to be accepted, if only implicitly, that the stages can be more easily delineated at the beginning than at later periods, but that is a characteristic that is true for the analysis of all language learning.

The Unit Credit Scheme type test is one of the more successful examples of criterion referencing which has come back into vogue for achievement testing in recent years. Again, however, it must be the case that criterion referencing can be of use only at early stages. Advanced language learning is simply too complex to state exactly what must be achieved at every language learning level (except in terms of broad partial coverage). Criterion referencing therefore, desirable as it may be educationally, has not found adequate support (and many would think should not, on libertarian grounds) from second-language acquisition research or from language testing proper or, indeed, from linguistic and psycholinguistic analysis and description to make substantive headway.

Proficiency Tests

Language testing has been much influenced in consideration of proficiency tests by Oller's research and discussion (1979), in particular by his views on pragmatic testing and the grammar of expectancy. The grammar of expectancy has more a psycholinguistic interpretation than a linguistic one and it might therefore be more appropriate to avoid using the term grammar and instead speak of prediction. Nevertheless, it is important to be reminded that prediction in language processing is central to proficiency, that it requires syntactic control and is at the same time not unlike a grammar in the sense of the combining of parts. Hence pragmatic tests (Oller 1979) are likely to use those techniques which combine the simulated procedures of real-time processing along with reasonably genuine texts. Dictation and cloze technique have so far found most favour as pragmatic measures.

General proficiency tests have been influenced only partially by this search for greater communicative validity. The Test of English as a Foreign Language (TOEFL), which has been analysed more extensively (Alderson *et al.* 1987) than any other proficiency test, has moved minimally towards a communicative mode and has changed only in terms of skill extension in its recent provision of a test of written production. Two tests which have been much influenced by sociolinguistic discussion of communicative competence are the open test offered by the Royal Society of Arts, and the British Council's ELTS test. The RSA test, the Communicative Use of English as a Foreign Language test, combines three innovative features. First, it provides for a profile entry and a profile scoring reporting. The test is available at three levels and in four skills and candidates may offer any skill at any level. That flexibility has, it seems, not been made much use of. Second, the oral interview is made deliberately relaxed and as much attention is paid to the interaction between candidate and speaker as in the Foreign Service Institute test (now the IART test). Third, the content of the reading materials in the reading component is intended to be real or genuine written English, and the tasks required of candidates are as authentic as is ever possible in a test situation.

The second test which has been influenced by sociolinguistic considerations and is in a different way experimental in its approach is the British Council/ University of Cambridge Local Examinations Syndicate's English Language Testing Service (ELTS) test, which offers both general grammar and general listening sub-tests and specialist study skills, writing, and oral sub-tests. The importance of this test is that it really has attempted to make testing provision for ESP needs and in terms of its evaluation study (Criper and Davies 1988) has been judged reasonably successful in this difficult area where language varieties are not discrete − as we have already seen. Indeed it could be claimed for the ELTS test that here is an example of language testing research and development having implications, however tentative, for linguistic description, since a major problem of descriptive sociolinguistics has always been to demonstrate systematic differences among language varieties. The conclusion of the evaluation study on the ELTS test is complex: it is that variation does exist among learners but it is not clear to what extent this variation is linguistic and to what extent it is psycholinguistic.

The IART Interview Scale (formerly the FSI Rating Scale) has received most extensive validation of any oral scale and represents one strong line of development which we have already noted in the case of the Unit Credit Scheme, providing distinct and clearly described stages of development for proficiency. The advantage of the FSI Scale is that through its wide use it has accumulated considerable validation information. Indeed the process of validation is constantly in conflict with itself since equal claims (in terms of validity) can be made both to maintain the same test instrument for the sake of accumulating data and to change to a new instrument for the sake of refining towards current views of validity, as we note in chapter 9 with regard to ELBA. As elsewhere in the field a tolerant compromise between retention and innovation is essential.

From time to time suggestions have been made of the need to negotiate some method of test comparability which would presumably allow for this compromise. Such comparability is particularly desirable in the area of production tests since without item matching of the kind possible in receptive tests, the equivalence of one oral test to another or one written test to another may be a figment only of statistical sleight of hand. But both ELTS and TOEFL are currently making attempts to stabilize and make more explicit both their writing and their oral tests.

Another recent approach to proficiency testing representing a deliberate attempt to inform proficiency testing with linguistic data is that associated with the work of Brindley (1986) and Pienemann and Johnson (1984) which hazards the claim that proficiency stages may be isomorphic in some sense with second-language acquisition (SLA) stages. Inevitably there are major problems here, problems of the status of SLA research findings and of their applicability (particularly when the data are morpho-syntactic only) to proficiency which, it is counter-claimed, may be as much a matter of fluency as of accuracy. Nevertheless, the issue is an important one both for testing and for SLA research. For testing the issue takes the form of whether indirect tests are in any sense equivalent to direct ones; for SLA research the questions that arise are to what extent the proficiency stage approach requires some kind of 'natural' order, and whether it is possible to consider it in terms of functions and discourse rather than forms only: and to what extent a natural order, if one exists, is relevant for any applied educational or testing concern.

Aptitude Testing

Language aptitude testing has enjoyed periods of activity over the last 30 years but does not seem to maintain a constant appeal. New aptitude tests are rare, perhaps because they are often reflections of a new linguistic or psycholinguistic model of language and learning. Even so, in terms of the influence of linguistics or psycholinguistics on test construction there seems very little change from the early Carroll and Sapon experiments with the Modern Language Aptitude Test (Carroll and Sapon 1958). The extensions provided by Pimsleur (1966) and Skehan (1989) are essentially *outside* language rather than deeper inside language although verbal intelligence tests (Skehan 1989), have on occasion been used to tap a wider range of language skills, influenced it must now be seen by sociolinguistic notions of variety.

Reliability

The attempts to make language testing more valid, which have been briefly sketched, can be summarized in terms of attempts, of a very similar kind, to make language measurement more context-sensitive, to move it away from the earlier fixed idea of there being one type of measure suitable for all purposes. The ELTS validation study results indeed imply that what is needed now in proficiency testing is not more theory but a very large array of tests suitable for different purposes. Of course the likelihood is that such an array will never be made available since the interest of testing and certificating bodies is probably in maintaining a near unitary test provision for the sake of convenience and cost. However, that interest may be met through computer-adaptive testing using item banking, although, as we note below, the form of item banking typically being adopted (making use of Item Response Theory or IRT) militates against variety of test items. In such item banks items may be differentiated by level of difficulty but not by specific purpose. The philosophy behind such item banks, and indeed behind IRT, is of a unitary competence persuasion and therefore not one which is sympathetic to LSP testing.

The search for greater validity through context sensitivity is not necessarily wholly desirable and the arguments against are not only practical ones. It is argued that tests represent or set norms of the standard language and therefore any attempt to extend the range of norms through different standards can be seen as divisive or patronising. This is in some sense the position of Prator (1978), but if the greater validity of more flexible testing always gained greater reliability then such tests would be attractive.

Much of the present development emphasis appears to be, in different ways, on increasing test reliability through statistical methods. That is a generous view of the present situation. A more sceptical view would be that the renewed interest in reliability comes from the increasing availability of computers, and the development of hardware and software. Thus Item Response Theory, most often in its most accessible form through Rasch, is used to produce test of very high homogeneity which are as far as possible sample-free (Henning 1987). Whether or not it is interesting or important to make language tests sample-free is a question rarely asked. It can be argued that sample-free tests are at the opposite end of the search for context-sensitive tests which more recent test development has been about. No doubt one view of reliability must be that it is one component of validity: this makes a strong argument for going on with attempts to improve reliability at whatever cost to validity − a seductive but dangerous view.

It must also surely be the case that interest in IRT comes in part from the wide availability of computers which, like other sophisticated machinery, have the capacity to dominate and not serve humanity. A serious drawback of IRT, the drawback of giving such test analyses maximum importance, is that IRT is really of value only with discrete point tests. But that is true also of current attempts to produce materials for computer-assisted language testing (Skehan 1988) which appears to be giving a backward rather than a forward direction to test development since the only tests so far available are very traditional and quite non-interactive.

Project Evaluation

The relationship between course or project evaluation and testing has come under strutiny within applied linguistics in the last decade. This reflects both the increasing importance given to process analysis as opposed to product analysis and the refining of tests themselves for more sophisticated (and therefore valid) purposes. Both influences undoubtedly stem from a general concern within the social sciences (including the language disciplines) for a less positivist, more humanist approach as well as for a greater concern with the non-determinist variation that permits individual cognitive difference. Such a paradigm is best observed in linguistics in the reassertion of the importance to language of social contexts and psychological processes and it is not surprising, therefore, that applied linguistics and language testing and evaluation have in turn extended their parameters. The effect on project evaluation has been to extend the range of observation beyond the outcome (and the entry−exit) test and to add to the array of measurements questionnaires to participants involved with input, ethnographic observation involving close analysis of discourse through transcripts, and self-assessment routines.

So much for process measurement. Product tests are still much in use, both integrated and discrete point. The intention of evaluation is clearly to provide as full a picture as possible of the project, course, or materials, thereby acknowledging our general awareness that as applied linguistics develops we become more and more conscious both of the complexity of language and of how inadequate our means are to describe and assess it. The extending of the types of observation used indicates our own recognition of the narrowness of any one measure.

The broadening therefore in project evaluation (Brumfit 1984b, Kennedy 1983, Beretta 1986) beyond quantitative to qualitative measures is another indication, in my view, of the growing maturity of applied linguistics and shows that it is now relaxed and confident enough to move with greater ease between quantitative and qualitative approaches to measurement and to be sure enough of itself to feel it is not necessary to have to choose between a positivist and a non-positivist approach to its own scholarship. (Chapters 7−9 provide a fuller account of the use of tests in the evaluation of projects.)

I have argued that language testing is of importance in applied linguistics because it operationalizes hypotheses and provides practical scenarios. Language study contains many primitives which resist scientific—experimental definition and remain at the level of imprecision. Language testing firmly tackles such concepts as *native speaker, level of proficiency, criterion, test, language,* all no-man's-land concepts in applied linguistic discussions and gives them definition and operational effect. By so doing language testing acts both as research methodology for applied linguistics and as data for model extension and building.

In chapters 7—9 we turn to a consideration of language tests in their role in evaluation. It would be clearer, perhaps, if we were to give the label *research* to this use of testing since it is not so obvious that the development of a test, the validation of a test, an experiment using a test and the evaluation of a syllabus should all equally be called types of *evaluation*. All are indeed research and/or development, no doubt. We will, however, keep to the term evaluation to emphasize the importance of testing in this wide area of appraisal. Neither research nor development seems a more helpful cover term and since both are recognizably aspects of language testing it will be salutary here to keep to the term evaluation so as to demonstrate our recognition of the important place testing occupies in evaluation.

7 Language Tests and Evaluation: Preliminaries

Circularity and Reductionism

Language testing projects have usually been evaluated but often not very well. The reasons have been various although the main one has always been the sheer difficulty of getting the job done. But there have also been other more local problems, the inadequacy of the tests used, the faulty timing and incomplete data, above all a failure to conceptualize the purpose of the evaluation. As we have just suggested it is not easy to evaluate, whether the project is to be regarded as complete in itself or whether success and failure depend on some external criterion. Furthermore, is there a process factor to be evaluated as well as a product one, and which has priority?

There is an inevitable circularity about all evaluation: the purpose is to evaluate, which is another way of saying to validate, that is estimate the validity of something. In the previous chapters this was usually a test, but here we are concerned with the use of tests to validate something else, for example, a language teaching project, such as the Pennsylvania scheme, the Canadian bilingual projects, or the Bangalore project. Now if the test is being used to assess the validity of a project, in the *first* place the test will not improve the project's validity. So much is evident. What it may do is contribute to a revised project which will in the long run prove to be more valid. In the *second* place the validity of the test itself may be in question, such that it is not clear that the right scale is being used. We are back in the dilemma we have already mentioned, that of the test–criterion relation and of the problem of always being convinced that a criterion (against which a test is usually validated) is valid in itself. In this case the project is the task and the criterion the test. We said (p. 40), that it may be that we must accept the circularity and recognize that a test may need to act as its own criterion. We are in the same fix here, for a test used to validate (evaluate) a project cannot ever itself be validated with certainty: we have to make our own best judgement and cut through the reductionism by accepting that judgement and relying on it. Of course we must ensure that any such test has reliability and that its own validity is assured in terms of specialist opinion, that is to say that it has content validity.

An alternative is of course to make use of existing tests for the evaluation on the grounds that they have more public accountability. Thus, a project concerned with, for example, the role of metalinguistic knowledge in the learning of the first language, the extent to which such overt knowledge actually enhances the first-language development, might choose to use a regular school examination as criterion. The reason would be that if the project treatment has any value it ought at least to show a difference on that common measure. Another alternative is to use an entirely new measure designed specially for the purpose. Note that there are again two problems here: *first*, as we have already mentioned, that any new measure has only itself to support it, this is the reductionist argument we have just been discussing; and *second*, that any success on such a measure could be regarded as non-meaningful on the grounds that the new measure has no relevance to learning, in this case of the mother tongue. The new measure would be dismissed as being irrelevant, not to the project treatment but to the first-language acquisition activity. The argument would go as follows: success on the new measure is of course bound to follow on from this treatment but that only shows that the students have followed the treatment. It does *not* show that the treatment was in itself valuable. To do that a different measure is needed.

Our choices are to use an existing test or to develop another 'new' measure, which would be neutral as to both the treatment and the non-treatment, that is to the existing syllabus which does *not* make use of metalinguistic knowledge input. It could, after all, be argued that such a treatment is of value in promoting some general first-language understanding or use. It cannot only be that such treatment is likely to produce metalinguistic knowledge in itself. That must of course be part of the argument but one that is so straightforward that it does not really require evaluating, and in any case it is concerned with evaluating the learners rather than the project.

Three Types of Evaluation

We can consider evaluation from three points of view regarding approaches to evidence: these approaches are cumulative. The first has to do with the learning, the second with what is being learnt, and the third with what the learning means. The three types of evaluation (Types 1, 2, and 3) can be presented as different questions:

Type 1

The first asks: are the learners learning what they are being (or have been) taught? Notice that there is in fact a prior question which asks: is any learning at all taking place? Although this may seem a trivial question to ask, it may be important when, for example, it is not clear whether the learning that is taking place is in fact the effect of the treatment or is taking place naturally or for some other reason. As an illustration of this, let us consider second-language learners who are learning English in a situation where there is plenty of input available outside the learning context. If we ask whether the teaching is responsible for the acquisition of communicative competence, it is reasonable to ask whether indeed it is the teaching itself that is responsible for this or whether the learners are acquiring the language from the environment. What this means of course is that under our Type 1 evaluation (corresponding to our first question) we need to restrict very precisely what we are investigating so that we can with some certainty assign the results to the treatment itself. Then we can be sure that the learning we are measuring is learning that has taken place because of the treatment and for no other reason.

This is one reason for including even for our Type 1 evaluation a control sample in that we can then legitimately attribute change to treatment. But that does seem too formal a requirement for Type 1 evaluation, which is intended to be informal, to be over-evaluating, trespassing into the area of Type 2 evaluation which we come to shortly. It should not be difficult to devise a test of items and skills that are unique to the treatment so that we can with some certainty determine whether the treatment has had the narrowest of effects, that is, to cause its own learning to have taken place. This may be easier to be clear about in areas other than language since a test of mathematics or history can with some precision restrict what is being tested to what exactly has been taught. This is less easy in language especially when – as in the second-language situation just referred to – acquisition is also taking place in informal settings.

Type 2

The second question, building on the first, assumes that learning is taking place and that that learning is of the treatment. The second question therefore, corresponding to our Type 2 evaluation, asks whether what is being learnt corresponds in any way to our general understanding in the area. Thus we might ask this question on changing from one type of syllabus to another, from say a situational one to a communicative syllabus, after establishing through a Type 1 evaluation that on our new pilot communicative syllabus our students are indeed learning. Our second question, therefore, is whether, in learning on this communicative syllabus the learners are doing what other syllabuses require. As we have seen, the reason for such a question (which might be thought to be supererogatory) is to accept that *either* the situational and the communicative syllabuses share some superordinate syllabus universal, *or* that the more powerful validation instrument or test should measure both aspects. Therefore, the communicative syllabus should cater for change on the situational syllabus as well as on its own. There is also the further reason that without such a possible comparison there can always be complaints that Type 2 evaluation is really a disguised Type 1 evaluation in that, even though the situational method students do not do as well on the communicative tests as vice versa, no one would expect them to.

In order to keep Type 2 apart from Type 1 it is necessary for there to be some provision for tests which are either neutral or firmly attached to the non-experimental non-treatment group. Success in either mode for the treatment sample can then be fairly attributed to the treatment and at the same time it is reasonable to claim that the communicative treatment is doing something both that is unique to itself and also that is being done implicitly by the other syllabus.

Of course there are always good public relations reasons for accepting as the criterion the *other* treatment measure, but there may also be not just good public relations reasons but straightforward political reasons. These may include the need that students may have to demonstrate within an ongoing state or education system that they have been successful − in the first place − traditionally. Only then will the extra, more modern, additional criterion be looked at and seen to be of value. In time of course it may be that the *current new* will become the traditional and the *current traditional* will have slipped away. But at all times change is as much a matter of social perception as it is of linguistic (or other) reality. Therefore it is important to accept that changes in syllabus design are likely to be cumulative and should be so rather than wholly revolutionary. This assumes an overall consensus about language and we appreciate that not everyone will be prepared to accept that such a consensus exists. We turn now to our third type of evaluation.

Type 3

The third question to ask is whether what is being taught is really what we think it is. In the present discussion this would ask whether it is communicative competence or communicative behaviour that is being taught. Notice that this is not the same as under Type 2 where we are interested in whether what we think of as communicative behaviour is different from situational behaviour. The fact of demonstrating a difference under Type 2 does not mean that we have syllabuses that are really communicative and situational respectively: only that they are different. In order to answer this third question about the nature of our putative communicative syllabus, it does seem to be difficult to make use of any testing approach unless, of course, we appeal to construct validity (as in aptitude testing) and develop a test accordingly on the basis of our construct of communicative behaviour. But such a test would be unlikely to be different from our neutral test of proficiency under Type 2 evaluation above.

Indeed the very act of *proficiency* test construction requires an appeal to construct validity because as we have seen there is in effect no content for proficiency tests and therefore no proper content validity. What is always said is that a proficiency test constructor must simulate a syllabus which can provide the content validity he or she needs. But this is tantamount to saying that for a proficiency test content and construct validity are very close indeed. Of course once the proficiency test constructor has produced a model of his 'proficiency syllabus' he then has real language material on which to base his content validity − unlike the aptitude test constructor whose data for aptitude test construction can only be abstract abilities, knowledge and skills since aptitude has no content.

One way of making our Type 3 evaluation accessible to a testing evaluation would be to use – precisely – construct validity. This would require a modelling of proficiency, not, as we have seen, in terms of any content but in more general terms. That would imply a more general and probably abstract view of proficiency since it would apply to language in general, not proficiency for one single language which is what is usually meant and required in practice.

Aptitude lends itself to this universal approach because it is aptitude in language that really matters to learners. What matters above all to them is whether they can adequately respond (through 'aptitude') to a developing language situation, not whether they have enough of a language at a fixed point. That is to say that aptitude is about process while proficiency and achievement are more concerned with product. What we want to know about aptitude is whether learners have aptitude, *tout court*; thereafter we want to know whether they have aptitude for a particular language. As Carroll pointed out long ago aptitude is aptitude not for any *one* language but for *language* (Carroll 1961). *Proficiency*, however is different. And it is different in exactly this way: it is always proficiency in a particular language that is meant – indeed general proficiency would probably mean aptitude!

We are compelled then to agree that for our Type 3 evaluation a testing approach is not possible. How then can we – if at all – operationalize Type 3 evaluation? The answer must surely be that we do indeed appeal to construct validity, but it is a construct of the project rather than of the test. That is to say that we fall back on the blueprint for the project, on its development and its reception, on expert judgement about it. What was intended? Does that intention hold up?

What this means is that Type 3 evaluation is unlikely to be satisfactory in itself: except in so far as an evaluator will provide a separate judgement from the original designer and that is wholly good. Type 3 evaluation ought surely to be in addition to Type 2 just as Type 2 should be in addition to Type 1. Of course any one type can stand alone, but if they do so they are open to the criticism that they are incomplete: Type 1 alone will be said to lack judgements about what it is that is being learnt and simply be self-proving; Type 2 alone can be said to lack a philosophical or linguistic view of – to continue our example – communication and again to be too closely tied to the project (for Type 1 too closely tied to the learners, for Type 2 too closely tied to the materials). Type 3 alone is surprisingly quite resilient but what it lacks is not this overall view, which it has, but rather the empirical support which measurement can give. Good project evaluation therefore is likely to contain aspects of all three types.

Let me give a specific example referring to our own Bangalore evaluation (Beretta and Davies 1985). I will not here repeat the details of the findings but consider the argument of how to set about an evaluation, and, in doing so, indicate, I hope, that there remain real difficulties which may in the end not be removable. Observe that I am taking for granted that testing is central to project evaluation. There are other ways (we have mentioned one under our Type 3 discussion above) which are particularly concerned with the theoretical modelling which the project implies. No doubt it is possible to make use of follow-up studies of those who have received the treatment and presumably those who have not, but notice that we are now very near, once again, a testing mode since we would need to agree on how exactly to carry out our follow-up studies, and in what ways to determine success. This can be done in a more global way through examining and analysing features of the discourse and other language use of those who have received the communicative treatment and those who have not. But for our present purposes we are concerned with the use of language testing in evaluation studies. Therefore suggestions that in the evaluation of the Bangalore project it would have been more sensible not to use tests are for the purposes of this discussion irrelevant.

Bangalore/Madras Project Evaluation

The Bangalore/Madras scheme had been in progress for some years, in a number of different schools and indeed in several localities, of which Bangalore and Madras were the most prominent. A number of different schools had taken part and in none of them when the evaluation started had there been any control classes. Why should there have been? The project had not started off as an experiment in any sense, but rather as an exciting development which fired the enthusiasm of people and attracted a lot of interest. Building in an evaluation design from the outset might have been desirable, with hindsight, but at the outset it would have seemed both presumptuous and deadening, and it was not done.

As a result of the considerable interest in the project it became important to consider the issue of evaluation. Even if the project itself was not making claims on behalf of itself, claims were being made on its behalf, claiming that language could be learnt in this 'process' way, that here was a communicative or communicational approach that 'worked', that it worked even in the most deprived, disadvantaged settings. There were also myths about it, that it required no materials, no staging, and no linguistic or language syllabus of any kind. Both for the sake of its friends and its enemies it became necessary for the main organizers to accept an evaluation, and preferably an outside evaluator (Davies 1983b).

I was asked to act as evaluator and undertook to do this with the assistance of Alan Beretta, at that time a PhD student under my supervision in the University of Edinburgh. First of all I spent some time observing the project (including the teaching in the schools) in action. Then Alan Beretta and I together developed in Edinburgh a design for the evaluation and he spent a period of about 3 months in South India actually implementing the instrumental part of the evaluation. We then carried out the analysis of the results and wrote a joint report. The aspect of most interest to our present discussion in that evaluation is its design and we come to that shortly.

We considered that the project treatment was so different from the normal structural English teaching in the South Indian schools where the project was in operation (never more than in two classes in one school), that we did need some basis of comparison, a bench-mark of some kind. We decided therefore that our tests would be carried out both in the treatment classes and in 'matched' control classes in the same schools. But which tests?

We decided that each approach (experimental/treatment and control) should be tested in its own terms on the grounds that if that was not done then it would be possible to claim either that one side had been unfairly treated or that one side had not been properly represented. (What after all would be the use of a comparison with a control group which was useless even as a control!) In other words we agreed on a Type 1 evaluation (see above) for both groups.

We also agreed that we needed a measure or set of measures for a more general assessment which tried to be neutral as to method, that is, equally fair to both groups. It was necessary to show that each group could demonstrate their learning on our Type 1 evaluation but this was not going to be sufficient since that would show nothing about the relative merits of the two methods. After all the Bangalore Project was there because it was believed that communicational/communicative teaching methods were better in some sense, or if not better, at least as good. This we thought we should try to assess. We therefore devised a set of neutral tests which attempted to assess the language ability of these children in both experimental and control classes without regard to the way they had been taught. Obviously this was not an easy task. How can one be sure of neutrality? And so we built in Type 2 evaluation in addition to Type 1. (We also attempted Type 3 of course but, as we have already agreed, that is less a matter of testing than of philosophical or linguistic analysis.)

Our Type 1 tests for this evaluation were (as is now clear) achievement tests; our Type 2 tests were proficiency tests. The actual tests used were as follows:

Test 1:	Grammar	(Control achievement test)
Test 2:	Grammar in context	(Neutral) ⎫ these tests were
Test 3:	Cloze test	(Neutral) ⎬ intended as
Test 4:	Reading comprehension	(Neutral) ⎭ proficiency tests
Test 5:	Tasks and problems	(Exp. achievement test)

There has been criticism of the evaluation (Greenwood 1985), especially of the proficiency tests, on the grounds that they were really achievement tests disguised but suitable for the experimental classes in that any type of test that veered away however slightly from the achievement type test we had used for the control classes would favour the experimental classes. If that is true it says something seriously negative about the control classes' method of teaching! It also means of course that those supporting the traditional approach (that is, *against* the Communicational Teaching Project) would never accept *any* tests as being neutral, and that leaves falsification of a hypothesis just about impossible.

Not quite of course. It remained open to us to follow one of our own suggestions under our discussion of Type 2 evaluation: that is, to use the measure belonging to the control group, *their* achievement test, as the main basis of comparison. If the experimental group could do better than the control on their own ground then that would be convincing evidence that the Communicational Teaching Project was not only doing as well as the control but also something different (and better). But such a view would have rejected our so-called proficiency tests and been interested only in the control's own achievement test. The fact that our experimental classes did not do better than the controls on the controls' achievement test was therefore a denial to those taking such an extreme view of the value of this communicational teaching approach. That way madness lies, because if the experimental groups had done better, there would have been a denial that these were appropriate tests. In other words there was no agreement as to the basic ground rules of such a comparison.

The only way out, perhaps, would be to use another of the methods we mentioned earlier under Type 2, that is to use a public required test, school leaving certificate or whatever which all learners must take whatever method they have followed. It may well be quite improper as an experimental method but success on that, doing better than those taught by traditional methods, would be very strong and public evidence of the value of a new approach – especially if it could also be demonstrated that in addition such learners can also do what their own measures (both our Type 1 and Type 2) do. The point is that those diehards who argue against any of our Type 1 and Type 2 comparisons could not argue against a public examination towards which they, like those in the experimental classes, are presumably directing their students (see Table 9).

Table 9. Tests in Evaluation.

Question	Focus	Test type	Validity
How much?	Learner	Achievement	Content
What?	Materials	Proficiency	Content
Why?	Project	–	Construct

We must remember that testing does not provide a discovery procedure for projects. The best it is likely to do is to show what there is, not what there ought to be. Description yes, discovery, no.

Tests in Applied Linguistics Research

We turn now to the use of tests in research recognizing that it is by no means easy to distinguish project work from research. Indeed in language teaching development it does appear to be the case that much of the research has been done in the carrying out of projects. It is also true that it is difficult to distinguish research into language testing from test development. So perhaps we have the following six-way distinction of types of language testing research:

1   research using test data both for test and non-test purposes (for example, the Unitary Competence Hypothesis (UCH), the Multimethod–Multitrait comparison; as well as aptitude testing)
2   research into tests and testing, using test data for test development (for example, TOEFL, ELTS validation)
3   research into methods of testing and test analysis (for example, computer-assisted language testing, Item Response Theory)
4   research in other applied linguistic fields which, incidentally, use language tests (for example, second-language acquisition research)
5   test development and construction (for example, the AEB TEAP test, the RSA CUEFL test, and also aptitude tests again)
6   research using tests in evaluation (for example, our previous discussion of the Bangalore Project).

We will refer briefly to the first four of these, which have not been dealt with so far, and provide outlines for their various methodologies. Then in the last section of chapter 7 and in chapter 8 we report and comment on these four types, giving examples of language testing research I have myself been involved in. I take the first four because they seem to me to indicate a ranking from central language testing research to peripheral language testing research.

Research using test data

Still the best-known example of this genre is that of the Unitary Competence Hypothesis. Work in this area has made use of a large number of language tests (e.g. Bachman and Palmer 1982) and has discussed their relationship in terms of correlations, variance and analysis of variance. Notice that there were two thrusts of this research, the theoretical and the practical, in that there was interest in the theoretical issue of language ability and equally (though not of course always among the same people) interest in the practical matter of the best, most useful and often briefest array of tests which would measure proficiency. As has already been pointed out, the results were always somewhat conflicting if only because of the conflict over which proper methods of statistical analysis to use: if factor analysis which type, *principal components* or *principal factors* and were the factors to be rotated?

The eventual outcome was, again as has been noted, that the unitary competence hypothesis could not be maintained on the evidence provided. But as we have suggested, and as was frequently pointed out, this method of argument using factor analysis had a built-in inadequacy in that factor analysis does no more than rearrange tests or subtests in terms of their intercorrelations. It does not explain or even describe with any finesse, and its rearrangement as we have seen has no principled basis other than the one that one wishes to give it.

Again it does not provide a discovery procedure. But much more important is that it takes for granted the measures that are fed into it as all equivalent to one another, whatever their differing methods. This is exactly why the Multimethod–Multitrait investigations were begun, to take account of the methods and hold them constant, so that any investigation into test trait, content or subject would show them up in a purer manner and not, as they always have been, contaminated by method. And so large-scale Multimethod–Multitrait investigations have been set up associated particularly with Bachman and Palmer (1982). As we have pointed out, the value of this type of research is that it has, first of all, provided more satisfactory evidence leading to some resolution of the UCH issue; second, that it forces us to take account of the role of method in our testing: this is a highly practical matter and therefore again as we have seen the best research in language testing allows for both theoretical and practical outcomes.

We have put aptitude in here as well as in test development. It belongs most usefully here because although it does arise as a practical topic from time to time (perhaps once every 10 years?) work in aptitude is essentially a theoretical question about the nature of language ability, that is, whether there is a special language learning ability which would make language out to be quite different from all other abilities, like perhaps musical ability. Carroll and Sapon (1958), Pimsleur (1966), Davies (1971) and, most recently, Skehan (1989) have worked in this area. Skehan quite properly and usefully makes the link in aptitude between the first language, the second or foreign language and aptitude on the sensible, but of course contentious, grounds that first-language ability is indeed distributed differentially.

It is interesting to observe just why this issue is contentious, surely because we employ different senses of first-language ability: what is differential is that aspect of the first language which is most nearly cognitive and which allows or permits school-based learning. An earlier formulation of this issue was offered by Bèrnstein (1971) in his discussion of restricted and elaborated codes. Of course what this therefore implies is that Skehan's interest is in formally based second-language learning, that is, in aptitude which is being related to first- and second-language contexts which are formal and school-based. How this relates to more general aptitude is left unresolved. Skehan's findings are that there is indeed a significant relationship between the L1 and aptitude and that this is related to the amount and kind of input received by the very young child.

Research into tests for test development

This is a very obvious use of testing research but one that is perhaps under-valued. A good language test requires a considerable amount of research and development and should properly be regarded as serious research since it involves quite straightforward research methodology, raising hypotheses as to what it is that will measure x in terms of y and then an 'experiment' that is a test trial to determine to what extent the hypothesis is upheld. But in addition to normal test development, which is what we have just been referring to, there is the rather more specialized but important and widespread activity of test validation (for example, the ELTS validation study already referred to, and the ongoing series of reports on the application of the TOEFL test worldwide). Another aspect of research of this kind can be seen in critical reviews of tests in operation, making use of their data and published results (for example, Alderson *et al.* 1987).

Research into methods of testing and test analysis

We have used as an illustration for such testing methods that of computer-assisted language testing (although it is not clear to what extent this is a method rather than a medium or a delivery mode). What we need to see is to what extent testing by computer does make a significant difference and if it does perhaps allow for specialized types of testing such as diagnostic testing which have been somewhat difficult before. Indeed there is scope here for a considerable programme of further work in the Multimethod−Multitrait type of research.

But there are more obvious and frequent types of research into test methods, for example into the whole array of cloze types and dictation varieties. Some of the more interesting research of this type in recent years has been into the C-test (a particular and rather recondite use of the cloze test; Klein-Braley and Raatz 1984) and into text retrieval for the purposes either of reading comprehension or of speeded reading (see chapter 9). In addition, there has been the spate of work in various types of scalar techniques for production tests, oral and written, and somewhat earlier in listening under difficult auditory conditions.

It does seem to be the case at present that interest in research from a specifically linguistic viewpoint has been overtaken by a broader interest in language use, in for example types of text, genre, register or specific purpose. The trend in testing has been away from the micro, the sounds, the sentence and the discrete point, and towards the text and the integrated. While the move is to be welcomed and in any case reflects (as language testing always does) moves elsewhere in linguistics and in language teaching, yet there is need to pause from time to time, and now probably is the time for some concentrated research on the relation between the more direct or the integrated test, which is currently enjoying a vogue, and the more indirect. We cannot afford to lose the language as we become involved in the investigation of its use.

Under this head we have also referred to methods of test analysis, specifically mentioning Item Response Theory. This is undoubtedly of real interest and importance among language testers and needs to be more widely known. At the same time it is important that we maintain a level-headed view of such methods of analysis and remember that sophisticated techniques are of value only if they actually do better analyses. We then have to agree on 'in terms of what' and it appears to be difficult in item analysis discussions to reach agreement precisely on this. Further, we need to consider to what extent language testing is different from testing in other knowledge-based fields (see the earlier discussion of Anstey (1966) in chapter 2). Even if Item Response Theory in one or other of its manifestations is of value (for example, in testing mathematics), that does not necessarily mean that it is of value in language testing. However, its advocates suggest that its major promise for language testing lies in the contribution it can make to item banking and thereby to computer-assisted language testing (e.g. Henning 1987).

Research in other applied linguistic fields

We consider fields where testing of some kind is used − or it may be instruments that look like tests. We need to be careful here because there is always a tendency to see a particularly powerful tool as all-powerful. It need not be the case that language tests are of value elsewhere and it may also be that what looks like a language test is in fact something else − an exercise perhaps, or in this case an elicitation instrument. The real question is whether language testing has anything to offer of value to second-language acquisition research and other applied linguistic fields. My own view is that it has, but of a limited kind. What it has to offer is the careful method of test construction which is typically followed in language testing so that the items in a test array are selected on merit and are carefully trialled for reliability and for internal test homogeneity. To some extent this approach produces the same effect which in second-language acquisition research comes from implicational scaling, in that it tends to maximize homogeneity of items under scrutiny, but is in effect a *post hoc* analysis. Second-language acquisition research could benefit, I suggest, from a more careful preparation of elicitation instruments.

All research in applied linguistics can only benefit from a wider understanding of the meaning and use of statistics in research concerned with learning and teaching. Language testing has always been centrally concerned with statistics for testing, and in many ways those statistics are also of considerable value in other areas of applied linguistic research such as second-language acquisition. This is where we come back to project evaluation since, as we have seen, testing is central to language teaching project evaluation; as soon as we start considering the use of research in other areas of applied linguistics we find ourselves once again considering testing in project evaluation.

Language Testing and Syllabus Development: Follower or Leader?

Finally in this chapter, I want to relate language testing to the general field of curriculum/syllabus development, using for this purpose an argument I developed some years ago in a paper I called 'Follow my leader' (Davies 1985). My argument was that language testing can operate either as the promoter of curriculum change or as the follower of it. In either case, I argued, there is likely to be an unsatisfactory outcome in that there will be an imbalance between the goal and the treatment. I give here an abbreviated version of the paper which argues above all for an integrated view of language teaching and testing, with each informing the other rather than as opponents. Then in chapters 8 and 9 I shall discuss examples of my own work in evaluation using the first four research types (p. 92) as main categories.

Reality for most language learners is socially constructed. However reconstructed the syllabus, the teaching and anything else may be, what the students' gaze (and the public's) is fixed on is the test, no matter how unreconstructed that is. And, understandably, learners are grateful for the social rather than individual reassurance because what they want is the reassurance that can come only from consensus; thus it would be possible to contemplate a complete mismatch in which the individual succeeds communicatively, interactively, but is dissatisfied because he does badly on the test which is out of phase with 'true' measures. Eventually, such a mismatch represents a lack of agreement as to what stands for the language. Examples of such a mismatch are found, for example, in situations where the syllabus and the teaching may be wholly concerned with the language, may be communicative, but where the test is still dedicated to literature. A student who is unprepared for such a literary test (which is institutionalized in the educational system) will not be grateful for a syllabus and a teaching method that make it possible for him to communicate with ease. He has not been able to unsocialize his view of what language learning goals in his situation are – they are literary and have to do with some kinds of language-like behaviour rather than with language behaviour. I want to go on to some specific examples of such mismatches and the harm they do.

A test situation such as the one just described is not satisfactory. Such situations fall into two main problem categories: problems of excessive conservatism, or problems of unthinking radicalism.

First, two conservative examples. One of these is a historical example which illustrates how a language test can become ritualized and irrelevant except in a symbolic way. The example is that of the 'neck verse' which is defined in the *Shorter Oxford Dictionary* as: '*neck verse* 1450. A Latin verse printed in black-letter (usually the beginning of Psalm 51) formerly set before one claiming benefit of clergy by reading which he might save his neck. Now only Historical.' (Psalm 51 – for those who wish to put something aside in the hope that they can, if it ever proves necessary, preserve their necks — begins 'Miserere mei, deus', or in our present vulgar or doric: 'Have mercy upon me, O God, after thy great goodness: according to the multitude of thy mercies, do away my offences.') The neck verse may be 'only Hist.', but we do still make judgements on similarly ritualistic foundations, for example the language question in the *UK Census* administered in Wales and Scotland:

Do you speak Welsh/Scots Gaelic?
(only recently added to by the secondary questions:
'*If so, do you read/write it?*')

Or this item from a questionnaire carried out in Bedford and reported in Sutcliffe (1982) — Sutcliffe was interested in the variability of English among the younger black community in Bedford and his questionnaire attempted to find out what percentage of the sample was able to speak Broad Creole:

The test sentence used was the Jamaican creole:
'mi asks di man fi put mi moni iina him pakit'
(I asked the man to put my money in his pocket). Subjects were asked to translate it and were asked: 'Do you sometimes speak like that?' A surprising number...said they did — 78%...Similarly, over 90%... reported using at least some Creole. (Sutcliffe 1982:151)

It is not surprising that Sutcliffe's results have been challenged, as he himself admits, for it is difficult to see *what* conclusions could be drawn from so unsatisfactory a test item.

My second conservative example comes from Saudi Arabia (personal information, Alan Beretta 1982) in the British Aerospace English Language programme where what is required is to obtain a 'pass' in the English Comprehension Level (ECL) examination. The only course materials used are the American Defense Language Institute's ALC (American Language Course). Over the years there have been complaints about and criticisms of this course but, I am assured, while it might have been possible to modify it in practice, the rigidity of the ECL examination does not allow for any change. Not only do the authorities forbid any change in the examination, but the students themselves know exactly what is demanded and insist that no changes in the course be made. Approximately 70 per cent of all items test the students' capacity to associate tenuously related lexical items, for example:

Stem: A *pioneer* was a tough man.
Choices: tradesman, colonist, cowboy, foreigner.

where the correct answer is colonist. The effect of such rigid testing is that pioneer, settler, colonist, explorer are taught as synonymous (known as *same—same* to the students) and that much of the teaching consists of similar vocabulary lists. My informant concludes that the format of the test means that there is no teaching of writing, speaking, reading of more than sentence-length, or listening to anything more than sentence-length. He provides this science-fiction scenario of a typical teacher–student interchange:

Teacher: pick up the book
Student: pick up same–same collect same–same take away
Teacher: start the next sentence
Student: start same–same begin same–same take up same–same commence
Teacher: OK that's enough of that
Student: enough same–same adequate same–same sufficient
Teacher: keep quiet
Student: keep quiet same–same shut up same–same quit it, same–same can it, buddy...

The neck verse and the *same–same* test both have residual validity. Those who were both poor and illiterate would not have been priests and would, in the absence of any kind of memorizer, have failed the test. Similarly, the *same–same* test keeps close to the ALC syllabus. What disturbs us about both is precisely the conservatism that characterizes them. They *ought* to have been changed, to relate to more valid ideas of literacy, to help revise the ALC course in such a way as to prevent what, my informant tells me, happens at the end of every course where students cheerfully proceed to the next phase of training, linguistically incompetent in English after a year (or often 2 or 3 years) of intensive study. No doubt it is a virtue of achievement tests to stick close to the syllabus. As has often been said, their job is to sample, and the validity issue is one for the syllabus, but without change in the syllabus that virtue of the achievement test is a recipe for disaster: the teachers alone just cannot generate enough power to bend those institutional bonds.

Let me now take my two unthinking radical examples. The first comes from Malaysia where some years ago the Curriculum Development Centre (CDC), concerned to integrate the two language-medium systems, English and Malay, as quickly as possible, introduced a new Communication Syllabus for English into the secondary schools. The idea was that what secondary school graduates needed was the ability to communicate in English, particularly in spoken English, and of course by *communicate* was meant that rather special view of communication which involves the capacity to cope adequately with the English of every possible situation. (I think it is now recognized that such a view is one kind of vague description of what the native speaker can do.) Schools were provided with the new syllabus: it was mandatory, and consisted largely of sociologically described situations (for example, in a tourist office or hotel), with no indication of what language was relevant or necessary. There were no textbooks.

The Examinations Syndicate, a separate organization from the CDC, were unwilling to radicalize their school certificate type examination to bring it in line with the new syllabus. The result was a grotesque mismatch in which the syllabus was in a large part unteachable because it properly required the competence and the intuition of a native-speaker teacher and the examination did not in any case test the syllabus. Failure was widespread except among those from the more elite English-medium schools; many average English-medium students and most of the Malay-medium students failed. Remember that the purpose of the new syllabus was to help those very Malay-medium students who had no access to English medium, and that English medium was then on its way out. Twenty-five per cent of the new syllabus was intended for spoken English, again to encourage the use of spoken English among those with least opportunity in school to use it. The Examinations Syndicate refused to give more than a token share of the examination percentage to oral English. The CDC had acted with brave but foolhardy zeal: it was right to be concerned about promoting appropriate use of English, but wrong not to check with its sister, but separate, examinations institution, and with the teaching profession. Change is essential but needs a Fabian lead.

The same comment can be made on my second unthinking radical example, this time from West Africa. In the 1960s, D.W. Grieve wrote an excellent report on English examining in the West African secondary schools (1964). He was then asked to rewrite the examinations, and at that point things began to go wrong. Grieve's interest in linguistics, an interest which had helpfully informed his critique of the existing school certificate (modelled on the Cambridge Overseas School Certificate), dominated the new examination which he constructed. Whether or not the new examination was piloted I don't know – if it was, it can have been only in the main urban centres, a warning to us all when we are sampling whole educational systems. But although syllabus and textbooks were redrafted and revised, the change was too great and the teachers could not cope. Of course all systems have inertia and some way round the problem of mismatching is typically found. In Singapore, for example, the Ministry insisted, with all the weight of authority, on reverting to a traditional school certificate type of examination so as to encourage in the schools (by washback) continuous writing in English which, so it seems, was being dropped after the introduction into the examination of a more objective-type approach.

Change in language teaching must be possible; that is, there must be some way of responding to new ideas and demands. It is best if the change comes in through the syllabus *and* the examination *and* the teacher. If a choice has to be made among these in order to move quickly, then undoubtedly the test/examination is the most sensitive; it is the most controllable, it acts overall, it is most difficult (*pace* West Africa) to ignore, and it has most certainty in terms of its goals. The test/examination is a major and a creative influence for change and development in language teaching, and if there is a need to choose then that is what should always change first. But the influence for good that the test/examination can have (and I would cite here the work of the Royal Society of Arts of London in its language teachers' examinations, its communicative test of EFL, and its examination in ESL; the Joint Matriculation Board Test in English (Overseas); the ARELS oral examinations; to some extent the developments in the Cambridge examinations; the work of the Assessment of Performance Unit (APU) at the Department of Education and Science in London; and the English Language Testing Service of the British Council/UCLES, the ELTS test; the AEB test of English for Educational Purposes), this influence must not be abused by moving too fast so that the syllabus – or for that matter the teachers – lose their horizon. Teaching shares with other professions a lack of innovative interest and is very quick to reject what it regards as theoretical, academic, or airy-fairy. Some 20 years ago in Scotland a far-sighted administrator introduced a new 'O' Grade examination in French and German, which was largely oral/aural, to meet what he regarded as the new wave of interest in and enthusiasm for the spoken language, for oracy as the important communicative mode. Those examinations still exist, still admit candidates, but very few. The soul of French or German is still claimed by the quite traditional literary examining, and teachers have not leapt to the bold new opportunities.

Most testing – in terms of bulk – does of course follow its leader: the syllabus, the teaching, in the sense that most testing is a check on achievement; it is *achievement testing*. But creative and innovative testing, starting often in a proficiency guise, charts a slight detour, not a whole new terrain, and in doing so can, quite successfully, attract to itself a syllabus change or a new syllabus which effectively makes it into an achievement test. Indeed it could be said that the proper accolade for a good proficiency test is that it allows itself to be outdated – it *becomes* the achievement test for a teaching syllabus and thereby permits a new proficiency test to be constructed, more appropriate for developing still more original ideas of language teaching and learning.

In chapters 8 and 9 we turn our attention to a number of studies which I have carried out over the years in various aspects of language testing. These have not all been published but they do reflect the role of language testing in applied linguistics and, it is hoped, support my view that language testing must be seen as a central aspect of the field, providing both a method of doing applied linguistics and at the same time a mode of argument in that it allows us to test hypotheses and also to encapsulate our ideas about the language (about language) and then try out those ideas.

8 Language Tests and Evaluation: Examples 1

We turn in chapters 8 and 9 to a series of studies which I have made over the years using language testing for some of the different research purposes described above. We restrict the discussion to four types singled out earlier. These were, it will be remembered:

1 *research using test data* both for test and non-test purposes
2 *research into testing* using test data for test development
3 *research into methods* of testing and test analysis
4 *research into other* applied linguistics fields which, incidentally, use language tests.

In chapter 8 we will consider in some detail two examples each of Research Type 1; then in chapter 9 we examine one example each of Research Types 2 and 3 and, finally, two examples of Research Type 4. First, then, I take two examples of work of my own in language testing, both concerned with developments in the Indian subcontinent.

Survey of English Teaching in Nepal

The first example deals with an English Language Teaching (ELT) Survey of Nepal in which a graded cloze test was used to compare levels of English proficiency across the educational system. The advantage of using such a test was that it was possible to make general statements about the overall standard of English from a comparative point of view since the test had been used with other populations (Davies 1987).

In situations of relative abundance (such as the UK) the importance even at early learning stages of maintaining a balance between the instrumental and the sentimental roles of education can be tolerated and accommodated to, in spite of the usual sentimental role bias. In difficult circumstances, in developing countries particularly, resources may be too scanty to tolerate such a balance and only one role may be achievable. Even in such cases, however, strong sentimental attachment may endure and obscure the problems of providing for the instrumental role. The official view may well be that both roles are important or indeed that the sentimental provides a necessary grounding for the instrumental. But, given in such circumstances the massive language learning death through school withdrawal after the early years, it is not cynical to infer that the reason for the large-scale enrolment in education (and therefore in language learning) is sentimental. Officials may therefore regard dropout as actual sentimental achievement, in that that the sentimental goals have been achieved early. So in these situations it may be that the instrumental role is effectively part of sentimental, rather than, as we might expect in a resource-poor society, the other way round.

Nepal is one such situation. The country is landlocked and among the poorest in terms of GNP. The literacy rate is about 24 per cent. For historical reasons English occupies the position of part first foreign language and part educational medium in the Nepalese educational system. English has been taught as a foreign language in Nepal since the mid-1850s when Nepal first came under the hegemony of British India. Before 1970 English was started in Grade 3 of the Nepalese primary school, while the few private schools were English-medium ones. The New Educational Plan (NESP) of 1971 made large-scale changes, aiming at 'counteracting the élitist bias of the inherited system of education'. English, seen as part of that élitist bias was started later, in Grade 4, and private schools were required to switch to Nepali medium. But before the NESP had properly got under way it was already clear that there were problems of implementation. More and more professional parents, especially in Kathmandu, were sending their children to English-medium schools in India, mainly to the Darjeeling area, whether or not primarily for the sake of English is not clear. Further, there were complaints about the standard of English in the state schools of Nepal and there were complaints about the standard of English in the university. In a small country, professionals can exert an important influence as a lobby.

The NESP became more and more difficult to implement and in the early 1980s it was finally revoked. Private schools were encouraged to use English as medium again and permitted to do so if they felt they had adequate resources, and indeed all schools were permitted to become private if they so wished. The intention was clear: to attract back to Nepalese private schools the children in Indian private schools and, at the same time, and as a necessary corollary, to encourage and promote better English teaching generally in the state system. Already by 1984 thirteen secondary schools in the Kathmandu Valley had been privatized and private colleges were also being set up. The population of Nepal had increased dramatically by about 50 per cent in the previous 15 years and the number of pupils in schools had also increased: between 1976 and 1980 by 100 per cent approximately in Grades 6 and 7 (lower secondary), indicating the problem for the Ministry of Education in finding enough teachers with adequate English even for the existing NESP start in Grade 4.

The Ministry of Education decided in 1982–3 that an ELT Survey would provide useful information about the state of English in the educational system and that the Survey should make recommendations particularly about the best starting age for English, about the aims and content of the present teaching materials and about the adequacy of levels of English proficiency among teachers. I conducted the Survey with two British and three Nepalese colleagues (Davies, Glendinning and Maclean 1984) and discuss here the Interview and Proficiency tests we conducted.

Officials and teachers involved in ELT were interviewed. One of the recurring themes in those interviews was that of the 'right age' for starting language learning. There was, we found, a great deal of support for starting English right at the beginning, in Grade 1: parents remember that English used to start there. It also makes sense to lay opinion that if a skilled activity (such as language learning) is not being adequately acquired, what is needed is more practice. Hence it seems sensible to start English earlier and to teach it, and thereby practise it, longer. This essentially 'political' attitude was countered by us with the available research evidence, that there is no optimum age for starting language learning, that adults can learn as efficiently as children, and indeed more quickly, and that what matters is the local situation in which the language is being taught. Here then we found a clear example of a possibly irreconcilable clash between political and professional considerations. For those making the political decision an early start has both symbolic and attitudinal support: the counterclaim of professional advice is not strong given that it typically remains uncertain and indefinite, remote and ineffectual. Our professional advice was that a start in Grade 1 would give too much attention to the early years and lead to distortion, essentially an argument against an overemphasis on the sentimental role. And with the existing English teaching force (as will become apparent later) three more years of English would not necessarily improve learning.

Another favourite topic was the 'decline of English' which meant that existing members of the establishment considered that young recruits (to the Civil Service) were less proficient in English than they were. We tried to make two issues clear: first, the difficulty of such comparisons over time, given that comparability is strictly unachievable; second, the romance with which we all look back at some better time, some prelapsarian Eden, more innocent, almost perfect. We all do it, standards are always thought to be going down. We talked this over with many people, and our results suggested that we did not know if standards had declined, but on our evidence it seemed unlikely that they had.

The instrument used by the Survey team for assessing English-language proficiency was the so-called *Proficiency Test*. This test, constructed by Clive Criper of Edinburgh University while attached to the Ministry of Education in Malaysia, consists of 13 short graded reading passages each containing a number of blanks for filling in. The total number of blanks in the test as a whole is 147. As examples, here are two reading passages from the test, the easiest and the most difficult.

Passage 1
Swami has a ball. It is a big red (1)   . He throws it to Lalita (2)
      she does not catch (3)   . The ball falls into the (4)   .
Swami can't get it out. '(5)   Tata, go and get (6)   ', says
Lalita. 'Tata good dog, (7)   my ball', says Swami to (8)
dog. Tata jumps into the (9)   . He catches the ball in (10)
mouth and swims back (11)   Swami. 'Clever Tata! Good dog!'

Answers:
(1) ball (2) but (3) it (4) pool (5) Go (6) it (7) get (8) the (9) pool (10) his
(11) to

Passage 13
His features were not good nor yet too (139)   . He had rather full
round dark (140)   , which might have been called pretty,
(141)   they been set in a lady's (142)   ; a fairly large nose,
which (143)   have been masterful, and (144)   was not; a small
still babyish (145)   , usually open and revealing (146)   big and
irregular teeth; and a drooping (147)   than retreating chin.

Students are given one hour to complete the test. Scores are reported in percentages and related to word counts in guided reading schemes. In order to reach a level of independent reading ability (that is coping with non-simplified texts) a percentage score of 60 is needed. The passages are very steeply graded and as a result the test was particularly useful for our purpose because it enabled us to compare on the same instrument pupils from Primary to College level and also to include in our test sample teachers of English. Results for students and teachers and relevant reading levels are given in Table 10.

Two very clear conclusions can be drawn from these data. The first is that students' English is *always* very weak: it improves very slowly and in Grade 10 is still quite inadequate to cope either with the School Leaving Certificate (SLC) examination or with the demands imposed by higher education. This conclusion is driven home by the correspondences provided in the last column to vocabulary levels. What these show is that, even in Grade 10, students in Kathmandu are only at a 750 word-count level and outside the Valley are still at the 500 level. This makes the effort of teaching and learning English over 7 years almost vain. Even in Amrit Science College (where, we understand, only 1st class SLC diplomates go) the average score is only 41. Of course some students are able to operate at the 'unsimplified text' level because of the wide range of scores. But others are well below.

For effective work in science and technology it is essential for students to be able to read with understanding ordinary textbooks (which are *not* simplified) in English. Even in Amrit Science Campus for most students that is not possible, and for no students at all in our sample from Mahendra M. Campus

Table 10. Nepal Proficiency Test Results.

Students	N	Mean	SD	Level of reader (controlled vocabulary count)
Valley of Kathmandu				
Grade 10	278	12	12	750
Budhanilkantha School				
Grade 5	24	10	5	750
Grade 7	24	32	8	1500
Grade 10	20	65	10	Unsimplified
Amrit Science College				
1st year	44	41	16	1800
Out of Valley				
Grade 5	69	1	1	300
Grade 6	5	1	2	300
Grade 7	186	3	3	300
Grade 8	16	5	6	500
Grade 9	207	6	6	500
Grade 10	34	8	6	500
Mahendra M. Campus, Biratnagar				
1st year start (Com.) 'A' stream	39	16	10	750
1st year end (Com.) 'B' stream	25	4	3	300
Teachers				
Valley of Kathmandu				
Primary	2	23	6	1000
Lower secondary	3	33	9	1500
Secondary	6	51	12	2200
Out of Valley				
Primary	11	21	12	1000
Lower secondary	22	27	8	1000
Secondary	43	37	13	1500
English supervisors	5	65	6	Unsimplified

in Biratnagar. Only in Budhanilkantha (Grade 10) does a school reach an adequate level, but then that must be expected given the unique and atypical resources of a British-run, British-financed, English-medium, neo-public school in Nepal.

The second conclusion is that teachers' English – while better than that of their pupils – is just not good enough. Only the specialist English supervisors, and no teachers even in the secondary system, reach the level of operating at an 'unsimplified' level of reading text (and outside Kathmandu the secondary level is especially weak). This is in our judgement among the most important findings of the Survey since it explains so much else: the frequent use of Nepali in the classroom, the non-flexibility of the English teachers actually use, the lack of supplementary materials (because they can't understand them), the reliance on rote memorizing and the dependence on the SLC previous examination papers as 'guides'. Teachers of English lack confidence in their own English and therefore cannot be expected to teach English effectively.

Our chief preliminary recommendation about English provision was that there should be less of it but that it should be more intensive, starting in Grade 8. Why did we make this recommendation? For three reasons:

1   there is no incremental learning through the Grades
2   teachers' proficiency is inadequate
3   the instrumental role of English needs maximizing.

We recognized that such a solution is elitist in that it excludes the mass from educational opportunity to which English now has the key in Nepal. We also recognized that the private English-medium system would flourish and that the promises we might make to improve the teaching in Grades 8 to 10 so as to make it better than the present system were only hopeful. At the same time the present reality was that the system was *already* effectively very elitist; the private system is flourishing *now*. English language teaching in Grades 4–7 is largely sentimental and may possibly deflect from a necessary emphasis on actual language learning later. The post-Survey policy decision to start in Grade 1 (later rescinded) biased still further the emphasis on the sentimental role. It did so in two ways: first by making the *appearance* of reform more important than the *substance* and, second, by laying a more frail learning foundation because of the necessary increase of teachers with inadequate English. The Ministry of Education was, we recognized, on the horns of a dilemma.

The planning imperatives required some compromise. Ours was to recommend in our final report that English should start (as was already the case) in Grade 4 and continue for 7 years, and not start in Grade 1. In this way some reduction of the overstretched system would be achieved. Fewer English teachers and therefore by selection better ones would be available. We also recommended intensive in-service teacher training in order to concentrate on Grades 8, 9 and 10. In other words we accepted that sentimental and instrumental roles both had their parts to play and what we wished to achieve was a lessening of the importance of the sentimental role. Concentration on teacher training for secondary teachers would mean that secondary-school entrants should be regarded as false beginners, after their sentimental journey through the lower secondary classes.

Our major recommendation then was for a concentration of available resources for ELT over the next five-year period on in-service teacher training for Grades 8, 9 and 10, first to improve teachers' English and second their methodology. What false beginners need is better teachers, better at English and better at language teaching, who can adapt their teaching (and thereby their materials) to the levels and problems of the individual students in the real classroom. Designing courses for training teachers to be flexible in this way is a major contribution from applied linguistics to Nepal's ELT problems. My argument, based on our ELT Survey of Nepal, has been that with limited resources there is need to concentrate on the instrumental role of ELT but also to accept that all professional advice is given in a political context where it must be prepared to compromise.

Communicative Teaching of English Project: University of Bombay

My second example is taken from a more recent study in the University of Bombay where my task was to act as consultant in the evaluation of the Communicative Teaching of English Project. In this example the focus of attention is very much on the testing instrument itself since that was being used in the project as the means of bringing about change in the system. Universities in India are often large, and exercise their authority mainly through the examination system – very much a case of 'follow my leader'! As will be seen once again my conclusions in regard to many of the students were not very sanguine. The problem with situations like large (not all) parts of Bombay and most of Nepal in regard to English is that the baseline is so low that it is very difficult indeed for any real progress to be made. One result is that there is huge wastage; another that many students believe they know English when in fact their command is very limited. The two projects, the Nepal study and the Bombay study were different enough. In the Nepal case the interest was in the overall standard of English in the educational system: what one might call a language planning study. In the Bombay case the interest was in the construct of communicative ability and to what extent this could be said to have been encapsulated in the first-year BA examination.

In 1977 the Bombay University Department of English founded an English Language Teaching (ELT) Cell to give direction to and coordinate the teaching of the innovative College First Year BA (FYBA) course in English known as 'Communication Skills' (CS). The ELT Cell was recognized by the UGC and funded for three years. The Cell, containing university departmental staff and representatives from five colleges, took responsibility for conducting teachers' orientation programmes, for materials production workshops, and for training in writing the new-style examination papers. It has regularly made available two examination papers a year to the colleges and has produced two booklets of reading and testing material (Davies 1988b).

The Cell continued its coordination work for some years after the UGC grant ended in 1980, but has now been disbanded. Since devolution to the colleges in 1982 of responsibility for FYBA examination in all subjects, no *official* FYBA CS examination papers have been provided. However, the ELT Cell and its succeeding core members have continued to provide examination papers for colleges to use if they so choose. Most colleges, it seems, have continued to use these 'unofficial' examination papers. Since the university no longer maintains FYBA records, it is difficult to ascertain exactly which colleges have used which papers in recent years.

The CS course was first introduced at a time when the University of Bombay was considering the termination of the compulsory English programme at FYBA level. The Department of English argued that a new type of English course was needed, especially for Arts students. Their argument was that students needed instruction in the specific English skills required for academic study and that a specially designed course in CS would provide that instruction. As a result the university agreed to make the CS course compulsory for FYBA students, and proceeded in a normal university manner to lay down target demands for FYBA students through the CS examination.

Although some syllabus guidelines were provided, control over the FYBA courses has always been largely in terms of the exit examination. Over the past ten years suggestions have been made as to the kinds of materials and textbooks relevant to the examination, but in the main what most colleges appear to have used as teaching material have been specimen and past examination papers. The emphasis in the examination papers has always been on reading comprehension of unseen texts. The comprehension skills targeted have ranged widely but the focus has been on inferential skills, on the very sensible premise that students need to think their way through texts. Thus the courses leading to the examination have officially attempted to be more cognitive than linguistic. In so doing they have necessarily developed language use and language manipulation and facilitated growth in English proficiency, but they have at least tacitly assumed an existing level of proficiency adequate for the deployment and development of cognitive skills of comprehension.

There is (as will be observed) a dilemma, possibly even a logical flaw here in that many students, perhaps most from non-English-medium schools, do not enter FYBA with the requisite minimum English proficiency. To that extent it can be reasonably claimed that the CS examinations are most properly suited to students from an English-medium background, especially those in certain prestige (South Bombay) colleges. Nonetheless, the claim of the Cell, and of the examinations they have offered, is that all students need these skills and that a good CS course can help students acquire the necessary cognitive skills, while at the same time improving their English Language proficiency.

The argument of the CS Project workers has just been alluded to but it is so central to the evaluation that it is worth repeating. Students, it is argued, cannot think clearly: this is the case in all their academic work, but particularly so in the activities of reading and writing which for most students are entirely done in English. Thinking, it is maintained, is in part related to language. The argument is not that thinking is hindered by inadequate language proficiency (though of course it is − as all members of the CS Project would agree) since having adequate language proficiency (or indeed being native speakers) does not guarantee clear thinking.

The argument is both more and less general; more because it does relate to all language users, all of whom need training in CS, less because the focus is largely on reading comprehension. So the specific argument then becomes: in order to read with understanding an academic text in one's field of study, a student must think. Having an adequate language proficiency is not enough; training in thinking, in cognitive skills, is necessary. Furthermore, although this aspect seems to be considerably played down, the training in cognitive skills will at the same time improve the student's language proficiency. Thus two birds are killed by the CS stone: *comprehension* skills are improved among students from English-medium schools, so that they read intelligently and critically and feel that their time has been well spent and is not just a repetition of language improvement courses which they may have experienced before; and *language proficiency* is improved for students from non-English-medium schools (the majority of all college students, though not perhaps the majority in the South Bombay colleges). And, in addition, they are given at least the minimum of the CS they need.

The argument is persuasive. It is the orthodox argument for learning language through communication (for example, Prabhu 1987) and for learning English for Specific Purposes, that is, for all task-based syllabuses where language is learnt incidentally and not taught as itself being the task to be accomplished. However, the argument does raise serious questions: hence this evaluation.

Like all education investigations it must be determined whether any change in learning is indeed caused by the treatment. This is the classical educational experiment problem, but it becomes acute only some way into a project when as so often happens evaluation comes to be considered (it should of course be built in from the start).

At the outset of many curriculum projects (of which this is an example) the central concern is to change methods and attitudes, to give a new direction, even to reinstate hope. Whether it 'works' in the measurement sense is often ignored or dismissed as being irrelevant. This is in essence the appeal to 'face validity' because, of course, it *does* matter if learners are doing better, or worse, on a new innovative programme. We can mention, only to dismiss, the view that innovation for its own sake is more important than learning, on the grounds that experience of innovation and success in an innovative project bring about a change of attitude which is, after all, the cornerstone of all development, including language development. Such a view must finally be unsupportable because it does not deny that language *development*, however defined, is what the whole thing is about.

It is critical to test the claims of a project that its treatment (like that of a drug) improves conditions: if not, then there is no point in change since a traditional programme is very much cheaper and much less demanding. It is also less exciting, but that may not be a high priority. The first question then is the nature and effect of the treatment. Alongside this there are sub-questions relating to ways of measuring and controlling, all of which are attempts to reach agreement on a satisfactory way of getting an answer to the question about the effects of the treatment. In the present case the other questions to be faced are:

1   What does the CS Project have to say about those students with inadequate language proficiency? It is complacent to assume that they are being properly catered for. Is it not the case (and thus a quite general question) that a take-off stage in language (that is a basic proficiency) is needed before even initial training in thinking and cognitive skills becomes possible?

2   If there is *training* in CS or cognitive skills and not just an outline of the goal, of the desired outcome (in the shape of a CS examination paper), then the language of the cognitive training needs to be graded. This is another way of saying that the skills themselves need grading, but since they are practised in relation to texts, then the language both of the texts and of the questions on the texts does need to be controlled and graded, for otherwise students are being tested all the time, not taught. Of course, if the answer to the first question is that the treatment is effective, it could be argued that explicit training is unimportant. In correlational terms that may be true, but the CS putative effect would still lack explanation.

3   Related to the training question is the taxonomy one. If it is the case that cognitive skills are important then there needs to be agreement on what these are and an accepted taxonomy provided so that teachers can base their teaching on it. Otherwise teachers use their own analysis of the past sample examination papers and fall back on some gut feeling about the nature of language. Escaping from literary criticism they fly back to it in despair. Or they may use one of the recommended textbooks and there run the risk of authenticating another generation of 'set' texts, as well, of course, as operating different taxonomic systems of CS.

These are, then, conceptual problems about the nature and claims of the CS Project. For what precisely is being claimed? Precisely, it narrows down to the *outcome* claim: that adequate control of the necessary CS for academic study in the University of Bombay BA courses is shown by performance on the CS examination. There is, of course, a necessary additional question which is how 'adequate control' is demonstrated by 'performance on the CS examination'. Does it mean that only those who score 100 per cent (however that is determined) show that adequate control? Surely not. But the question will not go away (any more than it does with any examination or test). Just how much is adequate? Where is the cut-off to be drawn?

The examination papers/tests produced by the Project have in the main followed the *ad hoc* traditions of university examinations. In this tradition comparison of results over time is virtually impossible since there is simply no consistency of measurement. (Note that even IRT measures cannot overcome the factor of ageing test stimuli.) Each year (or, in the FYBA case, each semester) a new measure is employed − and in the last five years after devolution of examination arrangements no one appears to know how many − which makes any estimate of improvement over time impossible. Apart from hearsay and the informed judgements of those who have been involved from the beginning, there is no objective method of determining whether FYBA students are better or worse than, or much the same as, they were ten years ago.

Now an evaluator who makes such a stricture must also ask himself why consistency over time matters since what is surely of central importance to the CS Project is improvement, separate improvement, each year. As long as the goal (the examination paper) acts to bring about that improvement, then whether or not it is the same goal is irrelevant. In any case, the argument continues, whatever differences there may be between papers are superficial; the examiners make sure that the papers are similar.

That argument is exactly what is said about all university examinations. But it won't do here: it won't do because the purpose of the project is to raise standards, while most university subjects are concerned with passing on a body of knowledge. Furthermore, as we have noted before, there is the uncertainty about what is causing the claimed improvement. There are, as we have seen, two questions here: first, is there improvement; second, if so, caused by what? It is, after all, feasible that what 'improves' students' CS is not the course but something else. All the more reason then to be able to accumulate evidence and compare year by year, semester by semester − otherwise we are making claims in ignorance. Any future development in the CS Project must concern itself with, among other things, test/examination consistency through the use of parallel forms, piloting, and item analysis.

Throughout my discussions and other engagements I was very conscious of there being two groups of learner, the one consisting for the most part of those students studying in prestigious South Bombay Colleges, and the other of the rest. The first group can quite properly be termed English as a Second Language (ESL) students in that they function easily in English for all official, formal, educational purposes. Some (perhaps many) also use English in more personal and intimate domains, to interact with friends or even at home. This group have no language proficiency problem: what they lack, as we have seen earlier, is the easy use of language for the exercising and developing of their cognitive skills. For this group, the ESL students, it is probable that the FYBA CS examination (and indeed the putative FYBA syllabus) is just too easy, not stretching enough. In part, no doubt, this is because of the uneasy compromise of the FYBA course which caters for both the ESL group and the rest. (It may also be the case that these ESL students need a more intensive, or at least a shorter, more steeply graded, course rather than one which drags out for the whole year and may often seem to them to repeat many of the things they did at school or at the Junior College level.)

The other group of students, those from non-English-medium schools, while less well represented in the prestigious South Bombay colleges, dominate in numbers elsewhere. Although in most cases (not in all, because there is sometimes provision for both an English and a vernacular stream) they are English as a Foreign Language (EFL) students whose English proficiency is inadequate on entry to FYBA (and probably also at exit), they are expected to perform as if they were ESL students. This they are not, since the only substantial English input they experience is in the English classroom. In other subject classrooms at FYBA level it appears that the situation is unstable: some teachers will use Marathi or Urdu or Hindi while teaching science or geography, simply in order to get their meaning across more succinctly or meaningfully and to have it comprehended. For this EFL group the CS examination is almost certainly too difficult.

What we find problematic of course is judging whether it is the examination paper that is too difficult or whether it is that these students are not gaining as much as they should. But how much should they gain on an examination paper which is (or may be) much better suited to the ESL students? What we need to know is whether the FYBA examination and the CS course help them in any way towards that goal; what we appear to *have* is a bimodal distribution, an examination that suits neither group.

Related to the above examination unsuitability is the inadequacy of some of the examination questions, an inadequacy that would have become obvious had these questions been piloted. But such mistakes are inevitable; all test constructors admit that their creations are fallible. What is unsatisfactory here, as we have seen, is the lack of proper attention to piloting.

A much more serious inadequacy concerns the mismatch between construct and item (that is, the situation in which items lack content validity). It is a problem that arises from faulty task or concept definition when an inference intention does not materialize as a question or inference.

Related to this problem is the lack of control over the college FYBA examination papers. If the CS courses were of a piece with other academic subjects then it would be natural for colleges to take on this responsibility, but the indeterminacy of the CS course is so considerable that to add to it in this way makes problematic these attempts to provide a coherent push forward for inferential language teaching. Indeed it is not far-fetched to conclude ruefully that most EFL colleges have been allowed to sink or swim: they were formally part of the Project but not functionally so.

And this is where we see the next of our difficulties. The core team (formerly the ELT Cell) has always been substantially ESL with experience largely in that area. Indeed, there was some surprise among members of the team after a discussion in an EFL-type college between the class teacher and her class of FYBA CS students about the text they had been reading, that the teacher had had to translate her questions into Marathi. That is to be regretted but seems to reflect the lack of fluency in English among the EFL-type students.

Teaching large classes is never easy but if the subject is content-based (such as chemistry or history), then teaching becomes feasible and plausible. But when the subject is CS, when the purpose is not to present *what* but *how*, to develop and practice and rehearse skills, it is supererogatory to lecture, a pretence that the problem is being tackled, which is a huge waste of time for little return at one extreme and sheer humbug at the other.

CS class size in some colleges is over 100 in number, the reason being an administrative/financial one that salary payments can only be claimed by the colleges when numbers in a class are over a certain size (80+). Once again CS is treated like any other subject which can be lectured about instead of needing practice. I was assured that amelioration here is in the hands of the colleges; in the South Bombay colleges classes tend to be smaller, and these colleges take seriously the CS weekly hour as small group tutorial/seminar sessions. This is rarely done in the EFL colleges where the smaller class size and the fourth hour in small tutorial groups are very much needed, but the EFL colleges are poorer and do not have the possibility of latching on to private funds as do the South Bombay colleges.

A distinction has to be made between the three components of a testing project: the *idea of purpose*, the *scheme or design* and the *test in practice*. I was often unsure during my discussions in Bombay, which of these we were talking about. There was a sense of mystique about 'the Project' such that criticism of a particular examination or test could always be deflected by the response that that was somehow not typical or representative or a true example of the purpose behind the project. Similarly for the scheme or design, doubts about the efficacy or indeed the adequacy of the design document could also be (and indeed were) deflected by the same comment, that there was somewhere an *U*r-design lurking in purpose land!

A plan was drawn up containing a number of research questions to be addressed by a set of research measures. These are set out below along with an indication of their timing:

Research questions (expressed as statements or hypotheses):
1   The CS exam is reliable
2   English as tested in the CS exam improves
3   English as a medium shows an effect
4   Students approve of the CS course
5   Teachers approve of the CS course
6   Students think out the process of answering CS exam questions
7   The CS skills tested are multifactorial.

Three colleges of the university were used as the experimental group for FYBA. Two control groups were used: the first of science classes in two of the three colleges (science classes have no FYBA course), the second of a group in two colleges of a second university in Bombay (SNDT) where there is a compulsory (but different) English course. A version of the FYBA examination was used in a pre-/post-test design and the results were as follows:

Results:

1   There were significant gains for the two experimental colleges overall.
2   There were significant gains for the two science control colleges overall.
3   There was no gain in the SNDT colleges.

There were therefore two conflicting results:

1   SNDT showed no improvement; it was reasonable therefore to argue for a treatment affecting the experimental classes, for experimental classes all show significant gain.
2   The two science colleges do show significant gain even though they receive no treatment.

We chose to explain these conflicts as follows:

1   The SNDT result is very important, especially as a direct comparison with at least one college entry level is similar.
2   The two science colleges contained in their sample students of considerably higher general ability than those in the experimental group, as shown on the school leaving qualifications which are directly comparable. Table 11 shows the case of the results on the SSC in the two colleges with science classes.

Table 11.   Percentage of 1st Class on Secondary School Certificate (SSC) entry to University.

College 1		College 2	
Experimental	*Control*	*Experimental*	*Control*
59	95	10	68

In addition to the testing, a number of other measures were used, including content analysis of the tests, teachers' and students' questionnaires, evaluation of textbooks and observation of classrooms. The conclusions in terms of our original research questions at the end of the two-year evaluation project were as follows:

Conclusions:

1   The CS examination is reliable.
2   English as tested in the CS exam improves. Yes (with reservations).
3   English as a background medium does show an effect.
4   Students approve of the CS course.
5   Some teachers approve of the CS course, some do not.

6 It is not clear if students think out the process of answering CS examination questions.
7 The CS skills tested are multifactorial.

Comments

1 The FYBA examination does have CS as defined. These skills *are* relevant to academic success and are related to language proficiency.
2 The FYBA Communications Skills course does significantly improve student performance in communication skills, especially in the middle levels of ability.
3 It cannot, however, be concluded that the FYBA CS course is alone responsible for that improvement because of conflicting evidence from the control groups. There is indication of a general ability effect and of an exposure-to-English effect.
4 There is, after ten years of operation, considerable support for the CS course among college teachers although there are criticisms of some aspects of the course (for example, the question on perception of sentence stress, the lack of an oral/aural component, the note-making questions, the narrowness of the skills tested).
5 The FYBA CS examination assumes too high a level of English proficiency for many colleges and should be adjusted accordingly.
6 College teachers require more guidance on methodology; for example, through regular orientation courses perhaps under the auspices of the prospective ELT Centre.
7 Student opinion, in so far as it could be obtained, appeared favourable.

We suggested that detailed work was now needed as follows:
1   Revision of the FYBA Communications Skills examination paper so as to take account of paragraphs 4 and 5 above:
1.1 revising so as to include a listening question and a cloze question;
1.2 ensuring that in the reading comprehension questions there is gradation of difficulty and that the lowest ability colleges are catered for;
1.3 removing the stress question;
1.4 reorganizing and renaming the 'note-making' question in order to make it a more general summarizing question with a variety of formats;
1.5 removing optionality.
2   The provision of suitable course material and of a commentary on how to use it in teaching.
3   Recommendations to the university's English Board of Studies on the lines of the above.

In both the Nepal and the Bombay examples we made specific and, it is hoped, realistic recommendations. Such situations are difficult, but they are not hopeless. The value of language tests in these evaluations is that they act as a way of focusing attention, discussion and planning on the original and on the existing purposes.

9 Language Tests and Evaluation: Examples 2

In chapter 8, two examples of Research Type 1 were examined, both involving language test projects. We move on now to Research Types 2, 3 and 4 where our concern is no longer with the evaluation of a language test project.

Research Type 2

My example is taken from the validation study of the English Language Battery (the ELBA test), which we carried out on seven years of the accumulated data (see chapter 4). The interest was in the use of test data for the purpose of test development, and what we were able to demonstrate was that while ELBA was a perfectly satisfactory test within its own construct (that of the psychometric−structuralist school of language testing) it could be shortened without making it less valid, and it was in any case in need of either revision or rewriting.

The ELBA test

The English Language Battery (ELBA) was constructed by Elisabeth Ingram, of the University of Edinburgh, in the early 1960s. Work on ELBA began earlier than on the English Proficiency Test Battery (EPTB) and was more of a research exercise and less of a development project. Ingram was interested as a psychologist in the question of language proficiency and realized that a proficiency test would provide an operational definition yielding research data. It was only later (in 1968) that ELBA began to be used as part of the matriculation requirement at Edinburgh University, a requirement which continued until 1985. No changes to ELBA were made after 1968 and no parallel versions constructed. The reason for the lack of development is very sound, namely, to enable accumulation of comparable and additive data over time. However, from the point of view of test structure the need for that accumulation is to be regretted since there has been no possibility of incorporating into

ELBA any of the changes and developments in testing during the past 15 years.

During the 1950s and 1960s the major linguistic theory underlying language testing was structuralist. As was common in such proficiency tests at that time, only the receptive skills of reading and listening were included on the grounds of practicality (such as time available) and reliability (how to handle subjective impressions). ELBA conforms closely to this model of testing. It has two parts, Listening and Reading. The sub-tests in Part 1 (Listening) test listening ability, largely segmental, while Part 2 (Reading) tests grammar, vocabulary and reading comprehension (see Table 12).

Table 12.   Composition of ELBA.

Part 1	Listening Comprehension	
Test 1	Sound discrimination	N of items = 100
Test 2	Intonation	N of items = 10
Test 3	Stress	N of items = 10
Test 4	Text comprehension	N of items = 30

Total items in Part 1 = 150; time = 25 minutes

Part 2	Grammar and Reading Comprehension	
Test 1	Grammar	N of items = 50
Test 2	Vocabulary	N of items = 50
Test 3	Reading comprehension	N of items = 20

Total items in Part 2 = 120; time = 50 minutes,

Total items in ELBA = 270; time = 75 minutes.

Both Part totals and ELBA totals are then converted into % scores.

Administration of ELBA has normally begun with a Practice Test which contains examples of items from each of the sub-tests and which was not scored. The only change over the years to the ELBA exercise in the University of Edinburgh was administrative; the number of testing sessions at the beginning of each academic year was reduced and the length of the Practice Test shortened to reduce testing time both for students and for test administrators. In addition, the number of exemptions was increased among those new students who provided evidence of education in English medium.

Two reports were completed: Ingram (1973) and Howatt and Davies (1979). Ingram's conclusions to her 1973 report were summarized by her as follows:

students who score 49 percent (on ELBA) or below are seriously at risk. The proportion of students in this group failing at least one of their class examinations is at least as high as one in ten. The position here is not quite so serious when it comes to the final examinations, but even here almost half of those who score below 50% fail their examination. (Ingram 1973)

Ingram goes on to suggest three possible reasons for the difference in prediction between the criterion of 'first available' examination and 'final' examination (see chapter 1):

1 'students have had more time to learn English';
2 'many postgraduate qualifications are awarded only partly by examination';
3 'every year some students with obviously inadequate English withdraw before the end examinations'.

Howatt and Davies reviewed results of entering students between 1973 and 1977 in their 'Interim Report' (1979), which analysed results of the four years following Ingram's report. The data that were analysed for the Interim Report were assembled from three sources: the ELBA test scores, the biographical data drawn from the information provided by the students on 'student information sheets', and the criterion information carefully assembled over the years in each Faculty Office and recorded on the accumulative record forms. These accumulative records were maintained in duplicate and sent out each year for supplementing by Faculty Officers.

The intention was to maintain a record over the student's academic career in Edinburgh University, both of his academic progress in terms of the results of any examinations taken, and of comments given by supervisors in the 'Third Term Report'. The purpose was to maintain a check on the student's development in English proficiency over time as observed by the postgraduate sypervisor, the member of staff in the best position to judge the adequacy or not of an overseas student's English.

Supervisors rarely took advantage of this opportunity to comment on students' English. Data of these kinds are difficult to interpret, and we are left unable to conclude whether or not supervisors were in most cases satisfied with their students' English or whether they failed to return adverse comments. There is the further possibility that such comments are not valid anyway, that supervisors' judgements on their students' English are irrelevant. That is a view which we can understand but do not ourselves accept; supervisors' judgements of their students' English may be attitudinal but those judgements are nevertheless of first importance in that it is on the supervisor−student relationship that so much of the student's progress depends during his/her years of study at the university.

In addition to spaces for providing information on students' academic progress and comments by supervisors, the Edinburgh University accumulative record also had a space for information about withdrawals during course. One of the problems of analysing these data is whether withdrawal should be treated as a separate category (Success, Failure, Withdrawal) or whether it should be treated as a sub-category of Failure. Data were collected for several kinds of withdrawal (for example, illness or academic reasons), but in our analysis the only withdrawal category included was 'Withdrawal for Academic Inadequacy'.

The Interim Report provided analyses for both undergraduate and post-graduate students. Detailed analysis was provided in the case of the postgraduates, by far the larger of the two groups. Expectancy tables were set up for ELBA scorebands (in deciles), for ELBA Total and for Part 1 and Part 1 Totals against First-year Success/Failure; also for Total ELBA scores (again in bands) against Final Success/Failure, against Language Adequacy (a quantification of the supervisors' comments referred to above) and against Withdrawal.

The results indicated that the likelihood that an overseas student will achieve academic success is critical when a cut-off of 70 per cent in ELBA Total Score is adopted, that is to say that 70 per cent ELBA Total score may be regarded as an optimum cut-off (or 50 per cent of ELBA Part 2). A higher cut-off would be inefficient on a cost−benefit basis because too many students whose English was quite adequate (in terms of the criterion) for academic study would be regarded as inadequate; a lower cut-off would be equally inefficient for the reverse reason. Table 13 makes the point.

Table 13.   Expectancy Table for ELBA.

		Criterion	
		Fails	**Successes**
	Fails	Hits	Misses
Predictor		(50%)	(0%)
	Successes	False positives	True positives
		(0%)	(50%)

The optimal position for the cut-off score is such that the Misses cell (low test scorers who succeed on the criterion) and False positives cell (high test scorers who fail on the criterion) are empty. Such an outcome would assume perfect predictive validity for a test. The reality for language proficiency tests is quite different and typically rs of as low as 0.3 are quoted. Even so, sensitive locating of the test cut-off can maximize the prediction or, in other words, place as large as possible a percentage of those tested in the True positives and Hits cells in the diagram.

The Interim Report pointed out that there is a linear relationship between ELBA score and academic success and concluded that 'poor English is a factor of academic failure. It is equally clear...it is not the only factor. Both improvement in English through exposure and tuition during the year and the linguistic demands of academic study are variable.' In relation to ELBA itself the Interim Report concluded that 'the information accorded by ELBA Part 2 (Written) is more helpful diagnostically than that afforded by Part 1 (Spoken).'

ELBA results, along with students' characteristics, had been collected over the period 1968−82. It was decided in 1982 to run an analysis of the seven years 1973−79 only, the reason being that post-1979 results were incomplete since many students had not yet completed their studies and pre-1973 results were not available (Davies 1983a). The total sample tested between 1973 and 1979 was 1605. This was made up of 1160 males and 445 females from, in all, 195 countries and 98 different languages. The largest group was in the Arts Faculty (456), followed by Social Science (316) and Medicine (215). Veterinary Medicine was next with 183. About 90 per cent were postgraduates. Students were classified according to the criterion information described above. Of the 179 undergraduates in the sample, only 13 failed their university academic examination; of the 13 who failed only one scored below 50 per cent on ELBA on arrival. We concluded that on these figures there was no justification for regarding English proficiency (as measured by ELBA) as a major factor in success or failure for *undergraduates*.

Of the 1426 postgraduates, 170 'failed' in the various categories indicated at the end of their first year of study. Of these 73 were reported by their supervisors as having inadequate English; seventy-eight withdrew on the grounds of academic inadequacy, and there were 147 withdrawals for other reasons − and it is possible that some of these were disguised academic inadequacy.

As is shown in Table 14 at the end of the first postgraduate year (n = 900) the proportion of failures (including inadequate language and withdrawals) in all scorebands under 60 per cent is higher than the proportion for all post-graduate students. In scorebands above 60 per cent the reverse is the case (the appropriate cut-off for Withdrawal in fact is 70 per cent). In other words a cut-off of 60 per cent on ELBA Total (70 per cent in the case of Withdrawal) is an indication that a student is likely to have adequate English proficiency.

Table 14. Faculties by ELBA Test Means of Successes and Failures.

Faculty	Successes		Failures	
	n	Mean	n	Mean
Total	900		61	
Arts	279	78.1	15	70.8
Divinity	29	58.0	1	84.0
Law	16	70.0	2	55.0
Medicine	112	72.1	10	67.2
Science	141	63.6	7	52.6
Social Science	172	65.5	18	57.5
Vet Medicine	151	66.2	8	53.7

Table 14 presents the ELBA Successes and Failures Mean for the larger Faculties. As expected, Arts requires a higher mean level for success. One of the curiosities which Table 14 does not show, is that a student from one mother-tongue background can be rated as adequate by one supervisor while a student from another mother-tongue background can be rated as inadequate by another supervisor, both students having the same or similar ELBA scores. Of course there is much hidden here, but it does suggest that supervisors do judge subjectively – and indeed how else could they or should they? – and that different disciplines and departments may well require differing amounts of English, a point made before. A few examples make the point (see Table 15). Another possibility is that we employ different standards for students from different mother tongues, that is, we have greater expectations for, say, a German speaking English than for a Farsi speaker.

Table 15.   Crossover Scores for ELBA Success and Failure

Adverse comment		ELBA score		Positive comment
Nepalese	61		61	Portuguese
German	59		59	Farsi
Icelandic	59		59	Greek
Hindi	62		57	Indonesian

Reliability figures for the test have always been found to be respectable (the manual gives figures of 0.93, for Part 1, 0.96 for Part 2 and 0.97 for Total). Indeed the Standard Errors (Part 1, 0.57; Part 2, 0.47; Total, 0.98) corroborate these high reliabilities.

ELBA is a good test of its type. Both its internal analysis and its efficiency in indicating students' levels of proficiency at entry to the university (as described above) are satisfactory. On the evidence ELBA itself provides it seems to be the case that differential amounts of English *may* be required for different purposes. ELBA is not very efficient for fine adjustments of this kind and certainly not if, as is now frequently argued, different kinds of English are needed. No doubt it was, in part, evidence of this kind, however non-explicit, that led to the development of specific purpose tests such as ELTS.

Research Type 3

The example I choose to illustrate this type of research activity in language testing is some work I have been doing over a number of years into *reading speed*. This a contentious issue theoretically in that it is sometimes maintained that reading speed is not a relevant skill in theoretical terms since it cannot be factorially separated from comprehension. In practical terms it is indeed the case that speed is of crucial importance in differentiating among students who need to read a large number of texts. This can be a serious problem for postgraduate students using English as a second language as the medium of instruction. As will be seen, there is the further problem of whether the testing method advocated in this discussion is one that is accepted as being a measure of reading speed.

Testing reading speed

A distinction is commonly made between speed and power tests. The items in a speed test are intended to be of equal difficulty (or at least within the capacity of all testees) and answer gaps then will appear at the end of the test, all early answered items being correct and the discrimination among testees made by finishing or not finishing. Items in a power test all discriminate and answer gaps (or errors) therefore appear at all points in the test and not only (or perhaps not mainly) at the end. A caveat is required in that, because it is usual to present items in a power test in order of difficulty (that is as a graded test), it is likely that more gaps (or errors) will appear towards the end of a power test, thus removing at least in part its major formal difference from a speed test. Nonetheless, it is the case that in principle all candidates have time enough to complete a power test and not all candidates have time enough to complete a speed test.

Whether or not tests should be speeded (other than those concerned with skills which are intrinsically speed skills, such as reading rate or speed, or component assembly) is a matter of theoretical dispute. The weight of psychological opinion (Cronbach 1961) appears to be that speed is irrelevant to cognitive tasks and that all tests should therefore be power tests. Eysenck (1953) disagrees and has argued that speed of perception and of processing is an important higher cognitive skill.

What is clear is that a reading speed test has by its nature to be speeded. What speeding means in such a test is what we have already defined it as being: providing test items in a series which cannot be completed by all testees *solely* for reason of lack of time. But the speeded element in a reading speed test is not an isolated ability in that it must subsume comprehension. In other words, a reading speed test must incorporate a reading comprehension test, however indirectly the comprehension is tested. Any alternative must fail since there is no value in fast reading without comprehension. Reading speed tests therefore incorporate *both* power *and* speed, and in speeding the power factor is responsibly maintained (Davies 1989).

To what extent tests in other fields, where speed is intrinsic to the skill (I am not here concerned with speeded power tests in which speed is introduced as an extra means of discrimination), maintain both speed and comprehension of the content of the task at a level of equal importance I do not know. Manual tasks such as knitting and other handcrafts may be relevant, but in many instances it can only be power alone (for example, musical performance) or speed alone (for example, athletics track events) that is maximized. Of course it must be the case that speed is a function of power in many beginning stages, in the sense that control, however partial, is necessary before rate can be increased. But the question I raise here is whether at intermediate and advanced stages of skill control is thought to reside in performing a task with both understanding and with speed.

One complication of speed in reading may be *flexibility*. This is so because fluent reading (in both first language and second language) is reckoned to operate flexibly, with relative reading rates (Wright 1968). If flexibility is desirable then variability is what needs testing rather than speed. Or is it? Surely it is *both*, since speed (as exemplified in scanning and skimming) may be a valuable reading technique on certain texts for given individuals and, in any case, it is necessary on some texts for all individuals. In other words, speed must be part of the desired flexibility for all readers: we maintain that variable speed is part of reading fluency. The problem then is to determine on *which* texts since it is likely to be the case that variability is, as we have just noted, individually constructed. In other words, it is problematic to select texts for a reading speed test which are widely appropriate. Reading speed materials which teach readers to read faster face the same problem in that they cannot be more than tentatively appropriate for individual use. This is yet one more example of the general pedagogical problem of selecting specific texts which have adequate generality, as we saw in our ESP discussion (chapter 6).

Gibson and Levin (1976:539ff) provide a useful critique of fast or speed reading schemes and materials. They refer to 'innumerable studies relating rate and comprehension (which) have come up with correlations ranging from -0.47 to $+0.96$'. But they also say: 'all the available evidence leads to the conclusion that learning to read at very rapid rates does not increase comprehension, if anything the opposite. But there are many occasions when skimming or scanning are appropriate, and if a reader finds it difficult to accommodate his rate to his purpose and the difficulty of the text, there is reason to think that practice, guided or self-instructed, can help. Many educators have emphasized, however, that variability in rate is not the cause of flexibility in reading styles, but a result of mature reading skill.' (1976:548). They quote Tinker (1965:7) with approval: 'the best way to begin a program for increasing speed is first to remove causes of slow reading: too small a sight vocabulary, weakness in vocabulary knowledge and comprehension; word recognition difficulties, over analysis, insufficient use of context, lack of phrasing, and vocalization'. And they conclude: 'no amount of practice can make us perceive what we do not look at'. (1976:549). It was in part this emphasis on the importance of getting at and teasing out the 'causes of slow reading' and on the importance of understanding what is read that led to the use of text retrieval (or text interruption, or doctored or mutilated text − or negative cloze) as a measure of reading speed.

Della Piana and Endo (1973:905) reckon that reading speed is not of theoretical interest and that improvement in comprehension in any case leads to increased speed: 'the most important issue is that of maintaining higher rates and of flexibility in rates of comprehension for different purposes'. They also conclude that extreme emphasis on rate can certainly improve rate – but at the expense of comprehension.

To what extent in a reading speed test the power (comprehension) element must be directly addressed is a major concern of this report. There are perhaps two chief methods of measuring reading speed. (I ignore such *ad hoc* methods as asking the reader where he or she has reached, either by saying or by marking the place.) The *first* is that mentioned above, the speeded-power comprehension test, in which the measure is the number of items responded to, counting from the first item (since as we have seen it is 'normal' for all items to be of equal difficulty). In order to ensure that the test is a test of speed reading (through comprehension) rather than a (speeded) power test it is likely that the text to be read will be interrupted with appropriate comprehension questions, such as:

$$Text: Q^1, Q^2, Q^3, \ldots Text: Q^4, Q^5, Q^6, \ldots Text: Q^7, Q^8, Q^9, \ldots Text: Q^{10}, Q^{11}, Q^{12}, \ldots \text{and so on} \ldots$$

the reading speed score being the question number reached by the testee. The type of comprehension question used is irrelevant for our present discussion as long as it maintains the acceptable level of validity we have referred to.

A variant of the first method is to ask the testee to provide a summary of the text(s) read up to the point of closure. While this creates, of course, problems of production assessment nevertheless it does provide a valid indication of the place reached in the set time in a text which has been well selected.

The *second* method is to direct in some way the testee's perception actually *during* the process of reading. No doubt it would be possible to use a classical cloze test with a limited time, but focus here would again be on comprehension so that it is likely that such a test would be a (speeded) power test. One alternative, which in my view maximizes speed but still includes power/comprehension, is the doctored text (variously known as text retrieval, cloze elide or negative cloze) which is, it must be admitted, a very indirect method of testing comprehension but which does surely draw on a potential comprehension of the test text even though that potential is not necessarily instantiated. While cloze deletes text, text retrieval adds text: the measure therefore is the number of added words (since the addition, for randomization purposes, is typically of isolated words) correctly deleted.

As we shall see, it remains an open question as to what extent such a test method wholly captures the speed–power distinction referred to above since it is indeed the case that the array of correct responses in testees' booklets commonly shows gaps (non-responses as well as errors) at all places in the running text and not only (as in the canonical speed test) in the later part(s). The argument for such a test of reading speed, however, remains: that the gaps (non-responses to test items) in early parts are induced not by lack of power but by excess of speed. I confess that this is no more than a hazarded belief, although it is an issue open in some respect to proof given that native speakers, offered a test of this format, typically do respond in a classical speeded way by getting early items right, and non-native speakers given open-ended time do the same.

I first used this method in 1964 as part of the first version of the test I constructed for the British Council (the English Proficiency Test Battery or EPTB). It was eventually included in the Short Version of the EPTB, the test actually put into field operation, as an optional part, and it appeared in all four versions of the test up to 1980 when the EPTB was replaced by ELTS.

Although its concern was with what many thought (and perhaps still think) to be a skill of central importance to foreign students in UK higher education (the population for which the EPTB was designed and with whom it was used between 1966 and 1980) it was, being optional, not much used. The technique has not, as far as I am aware, aroused much interest. The only reference to it I have met is that of Winton Manning and his CALL cloze elide system (Manning 1987). I made a brief reference to it myself (Davies 1975) comparing the reading speed test (known in EPTB as test 5) with the EPTB test of modified cloze (test 3):

> Test 3's r of 0.5, 0.6, 0.7 with test 5 has been quoted. What does test 5 measure? The technique here (after the practice lead-in with some non-English words) is to interpose English distractors randomly in a running text. Testees are asked to mark (circle) these distractors while 'reading' the text as fast as they can. They are stopped at the end of 10 minutes, and the number of distractors located is their raw score. There is a deduction for each non distractor marked (but not more than 4 deductions in any one line of the original text). Again the validity figures. . .have the same range (0.4 to 0.7) as test 3. Its range of correlations with test 3 has already been quoted. Its reliability has always been above 0.9. Its mean is 70 and its standard deviation is 33. . .
>
> Does test 5 test reading speed?. . .the relation of both test 3 and test 5 to test 4. . .a discrete point grammar test. (with) 47 items,. . .of the multiple choice variety (3 choices). . .traditional in format. . . .Its range of correlations with tests 3 and 5 is 0.5 to 0.7. We can say therefore that the mean correlation between tests 3 and 4, 4 and 5 and 3 and 5 is 0.6. Test 4's reliability is between 0.8 and 0.9. . .its mean is 33 and its standard deviation is 8. . .in the original factor analysis tests 3, 4 and 5 all loaded on the 3rd factor, which was labelled Reading Comprehension. . . . (Davies 1975:124)

There has never been much interest in the text retrieval/doctored text test method and although the original test constructed for the British Council was used on occasion it was usually avoided (it was optional and testing programmes always are short of time). A follow-up study in Edinburgh was carried out in

1987. There remains unresolved the basic issue of just how appropriate it is to assume that a given 'general' test is equally appropriate to all testees to demonstrate their capacity for speed reading.

A text was selected from a passage on early twentieth-century British history dealing with the General Strike in the 1920s. The text contained 236 words (see below) and into the text a set of randomly selected words was inserted. Two versions (A and B) of the test were prepared: the only difference between the two versions was in the place of word insertion. The same intrusive words were inserted in each text but for obvious reasons of juxtaposition prediction not in the same order in each version (there was a slight difference between the inserted sets for A and B on account of the need to avoid possible collocations in each version). The first inserted word in both texts was intended as an example to show the testee the procedure to be followed. In both cases the whole of the first sentence was uninterrupted in order to provide the testee with the necessary context for reading the rest of the text.

Original Text (without insertions):
The volunteers came in their thousands: not only the thousands of respectable middle-aged professional men who were queuing outside recruiting stations, but medical students, law students and undergraduates from Oxford and Cambridge, to whom the strike was an exciting joke. The attitude of the University authorities varied. The Vice-Chancellor said that it was not desirable that any undergraduates should enrol for service and that leave of absence would not be granted to any who were due to take examinations. This sentiment was far from universal. J.C. Nevinson, a student then in his third year at Exeter, noted in his diary on Monday 'the sub-rector and the Principal caught the fever early, the latter urged undergraduates to enrol themselves, the former gave a discourse to a crowded and thrilled audience who were exhorted to come and sign on between 10 and 2 tomorrow; persons with cars were needed, or those who could drive. The rest to be used as porters and shifters of goods etc. All remarkably fatuous and quite unnecessary for the unions are maintaining essential services. Nevinson discovered quickly that his opinion was not generally shared. Most of the college put down their names, including many who were doing examinations, which they hoped to avoid. 'I wonder when badges and white feathers will appear?' he asked ironically, but in fact he encountered no ill will for opposing volunteering in a college which supported it.

The instructions given were as follows: 'Read the passage as quickly as you can. After the first sentence some of the words are irrelevant. Mark those words by putting a cross through them. The first is done as an example for you.' Three places of word insertion were adopted, the purpose being to begin the examination of the equivalence of locus of distraction. Forms A and B were distinguished in terms of order of insertion location. The three locuses were:

1   after nouns (N); 2   after Verbs (V); 3   Random (R)
The order in Form A was:
after N (8 egs); V (11 egs); R (19 egs): total = 38
and in Form B:
V (7 egs); R (18 egs); N (13 egs): total = 38

The total number of distractors was determined by the tokens of categories (N and V) occurring in the text and some attempt was made to balance Form A and Form B: thus Form A had the following composition:

Sentence (S) 1 ⎫   : lead in
S2   ⎭   : example +8N and distractors

S3 ⎫
S4 ⎪
S5 ⎪
S6 ⎬   : 11V + distractors
S7 ⎪
S8 ⎪
S9 ⎭

S10   19 randomly placed distractors

Form B had the following composition:

S1   : lead in
S2   : example
S3   : 7 V + distractors

S4 ⎫
S5 ⎪
S6 ⎬   : 18 R + distractors
S7 ⎪
S8 ⎪
S9 ⎭

S10   :13 N + distractors

Forms A and B were randomly distributed to 90 testees (A: 46; B: 44) made up of three groups:

Native speakers of English (NS): N = 23, postgraduate students and
   teachers;
Non-native speakers of English (NNS): N = 24, postgraduate students
   in the University of Edinburgh;

Non-native speakers of English (NNS): N = 43, EFL students in a Dublin language school.

Testees were allowed 4 minutes* to complete the test. The test was scored positively, that is for correct deletions only. No account was taken of incorrect deletions or gaps.

Percentage means for each subcategory (for example Noun) are quoted; the use of percentages avoids differences between raw totals in each subcategory (see Table 16).

Table 16. Mean Scores (percentages) for two Text Retrieval Tests.

			Percentage mean		
		N	V	R	T
NS	A (N = 10)	91	94	87	89
NS	B (N = 13)	61	94	93	81
NNS	A (N = 36)	38	23	16	22
NNS	B (N = 31)	9	30	30	23

The order of category in A and B was, as has been explained, different. When rank orders for category success were looked at the results were, with sequential order of category represented by the display order, and rank order of success indicated by number in brackets (see Table 17).

Table 17. Rank Orders of Subcategory Success in Test Retrieval Tests.

NS A	N (2)	V (1)	R (3)
NS B	V (1)	R (2)	N (3)
NNS A	N (1)	V (2)	R (3)
NNS B	V (1=)	R (1=)	N (3)

At that point my conclusions were as follows:

1 The test discriminates in appropriate ways.
2 Order of presentation does appear to matter with in all cases the last presented category (R or N) scoring least. This is to be expected in a speed test.

---

* The average adult reads at an average speed of about 200 to 400 words per minute, usually nearer 200 (Gibson and Levin 1975:539)

3   There is some indication that V is easier than N or R (see Tables 16, 17). But this may be a reflection of the difficulty of N.
4   N is the most difficult of all three categories although this may reflect its position; however, although V is never in last position R is, and R is not as difficult as N.
5   Both category and order of presentation therefore appear to matter.
6   A third version of the test needs to be explored in which the order is R N V.

This was the end of the first stage. In Melbourne in 1988 I was able to extend the investigation to the use of the third version of the test. Form C was prepared in which the make-up and the order were as follows:

Form C:
      R: 20; N: 8; V: 10: total = 38

Sentences 3, 4 and 5 contained the 20 R insertions; sentences 6, 7 and 8 the 8 N insertions and sentences 9 and 10 the 10 V insertions. Form C was attempted by 9 native speakers of English and 63 non-native speakers. Their results were as shown in Table 18.

Table 18.   Percentage Means for Melbourne Sample Version C.

			Percentage mean		
		N	V	R	T
NS	C	97	96	89	95
NNS	C	30	23	43	35

The rank order for all category success in all *three* versions now becomes as shown in Table 19 (with linear order and rank order displayed as before).

Table 19.   Rank Orders of Subcategory Success, Tests A, B, C compared.

NS	A	N (2)	V (1)	R (3)
	B	V (1)	R (2)	N (3)
	C	R (1)	N (2)	V (3)
NNS	A	N (1)	V (2)	R (3)
	B	V (1=)	R (1=)	N (3)
	C	R (1)	N (2)	V (3)

The picture is now somewhat clearer and it appears that our suggestion that N is the most difficult subcategory cannot really be sustained. True, it does remain overall the most difficult for NS but that may well be a factor of lack of discrimination in what is for NS an easy test. In the case of NNS V is marginally the most difficult but again there is very little in it. The most obvious conclusion is that it is not category that matters but order of presentation. In other words, when category is controlled, *order of presentation* (with the single exception in Test A for NS) is what determines success. This is very much exaggerated of course in the case of NNS because the samples we have tested are so very diverse and, as a result, there is a clear tendency to leave large gaps in the later items. But this is after all *intended* to be a speed test, and we conclude therefore that the test of text retrieval is indeed a speed reading test. Furthermore, we conclude that this holds true wherever distractors are placed and that suggests that the process of fast reading does not prevent comprehension. If it did then the different insertion places might well provide for differential outcomes.

We move now from a concern with tests as tests to testing more widely in applied linguistics.

Research Type 4

The fourth research type is that of research into other areas of applied linguistics and I again choose two examples of my own research. Both relate to work in the general area of curriculum and, in particular, that of specific purpose needs; it is not surprising therefore that the second example concerns a needs analysis approach. My first example refers to work on a listening test for non-English-speaking medical practitioners seeking temporary registration in order to work as doctors in the UK. As will be seen, I offer here a comparison between a specific and a non-specific test.

Testing the English of medicine: direct or indirect?

In reporting on this ESP test my discussion raises what seems to me the enduring question of the relation between direct and indirect types of testing. It is all too easy to accept the specific purpose argument because it is so appealing in terms of face validity. What is more, there is obviously truth in it. The real difficulty is, as we saw earlier with the ELTS test, which specificity should we be concerned with? And this is not now an argument about types of content or areas of knowledge; rather, it is about more linguistic questions which perhaps deserve the name of genre: how do doctors talk to one another, how do patients expect to be addressed by doctors, what is the unmarked style of discourse in such settings? In our preparation for the listening test we tried to take account of such questions and although it was not possible to build in many of the findings into the test itself nevertheless the test is, in my judgement, improved by the work we did in preparation in the hospitals and clinics. Here then is the account of work done in connection with a listening test for the Professional and Linguistic Assessment Board (PLAB).

ESP teaching is by definition context-based, and similarly for ESP testing. The central ESP testing position is that proficiency tests should be performance tests – this is the philosophy behind the British Council's ELTS test, the AEB's TEAP test and the Ontario OTESOL test – that is, they should all be tests of contextual language use, using authentic or semi-authentic texts and genuine or semi-genuine tasks.

I will first describe the rationale behind this listening test project in medical English, and then query the extent to which communicative use needs to be sampled and/or predicated on a strong direct testing philosophy; to this end I will make a comparison with an earlier medical English test which is quite indirect. I raise the issue of test and behavioural identity and query the extent to which tests require authentic behaviour as opposed to imagined linguistic context, or, to put it another way, raise the question of whether language skill is, as we are accustomed to being told, more important than language knowledge. I conclude that, as Anastasi tells us, it is not necessary for tests to be behaviourly based in any simple fashion but that it is of course necessary for tests to tap linguistic behaviour in the required areas, and that this is precisely where professional testing expertise is needed, in that it *is* possible to *represent* an area of language behaviour in a variety of ways, among them a set of vocabulary items. Communicative language testing does *not* require that the tests themselves should be communicative.

A test of listening comprehension for non-native-English-speaking doctors seeking registration in the UK is now compulsory. An evaluation of the existing test, which was constructed in the early 1970s, commented on the importance of providing a communicative rationale. The design of the present test was based on a linguistic analysis of spoken English within a medical context and contains discrete point items of linguistic features such as intonation. Commenting on the well-known difficulty of testing intonation, the evaluation noted that there is considerable variation among native speakers in terms of intonation and, in any case, intonation signals are often redundant.

It was recommended that a more contextualized test was needed which would sample more authentically the work of a senior house officer (SHO), the criterion grade for the test. The SHO spends a lot of time on ward duty; the work is complex, medically and linguistically, much of the time used for listening to patients and taking their history, or discussing patients with a registrar or consultant, often by telephone. Overseas doctors experience mis-understanding because of their inability to latch on to the implication of what is being said, to get the drift in, for example, a case conference. Overseas doctors themselves often emphasize the difficulty of asking questions and the problem of understanding patients with local and regional accents. These are the problems of all non-native speakers since they lack flexibility. A listening test can do nothing for the first problem (which is one of production) and little for the second (because of the difficulty of adequate sampling).

The evaluation noted that changes had taken place in views of listening and testing listening and recommended that a new test should contain aspects of the ongoing and sequential context of ordinary discourse and include some items focusing on longer stretches of conversation in medical contexts so as to allow for the inferencing mentioned earlier and for the successful predicting that we all do when we are engaging successfully in a linguistic interaction.

In development work for the new test, considerable attention was given to the collection of medical discourse data in the following areas: doctor interacting with patients and relatives; ward rounds when the senior house officer is acting as assistant to the consultant; case conferences; telephone conversations between doctor and other medical staff. An analysis was made of the medical language behaviours to be predicted and the strong ESP position was taken up, that close approximation of the stimuli texts to the tasks (for example, inferencing) required of SHOs should be maintained.

It is, however, worthwhile asking whether such a strong ESP position is necessary or whether a much more indirect test−behaviour relationship is just as (or even more) appropriate. In his study of overseas doctors in the NHS, Smith (1980) incorporated a test of colloquial English 'after consultation with Joy Parkinson of Southwark College'. Much of the material for test items was taken from *A Manual of English for the Overseas Doctor* by Joy Parkinson, published by Churchill Livingstone in 1976.

The Smith−Parkinson test consists of 30 items:

1   10 nouns or noun phrases used in common speech for which there is an exactly equivalent medical term. In each case the interviewer read out the common term, while the informant was asked to pick out the corre-sponding medical term from a list of four possibilities (plus 'don't know'), for example:

   PINK eye: conjunctivitis, albinism, short sight, gordeolum, don't know.

2   10 colloquial or slangy phrases that patients are likely to use in the consulting room; some of them describe medical conditions, some deal euphemistically or crudely with sexual functions, and some express very basic ideas (such as being tired) which regularly occur in medical contexts. Again the interviewer read out the phrase, while the informant picked out the equivalent phrase in completely plain English from a list of four, for example:

   The mother said her daughter was full of beans:
      she was overweight,
      she was difficult to control,
      she was growing fast,
      she was healthy and energetic.

3   10 items based on common verbs which are used with prepositions, such as 'looking forward to'. The informant was given a list of sentences and was then asked to produce an equivalent sentence using the verb shown in brackets together with the correct preposition, for example:

I'm feeling in poor health doctor (RUN, down)

Most if not all of the items related closely or loosely to a medical context.

Reliability for the test of 0.87 (split half) is claimed. It is not clear how Smith scored Section 3, and in Section 1 item 5 was not scored. When I administered the test (Davies 1986) to 24 overseas students including doctors attending English and medical courses in Edinburgh, only one had a total score of over 18 and was therefore (according to Smith) the only one not at risk. The total mean score was 7.4 with a standard deviation (SD) of 4.8. The correlations (product moment) among parts were as shown in Table 20. It would appear that Section 2 has more commonality than Section 1 and Section 3, a point we will come back to in terms of later results.

Table 20.   Inter-part Correlations for Smith–Parkinson Test.

	Section 1	*Section 2*	*Section 3*	*Total*
1		0.668	0.163	0.881
2			0.337	0.861
3				0.554
Total				

Seven of the 24 testees had earlier taken the British Council ELTS (Medical Sciences) test and profile results for these students were available from the students themselves. Significant correlations were achieved of 0.715 (Section 2 of Smith–Parkinson – S–P – with ELTS Medical Test (Writing) and 0.857 (Section 1 of S–P with ELTS General English (Reading)). I do not say this in any way to diminish the importance or the interest of ELTS, but rather to raise the question (Anastasi's question) of just what are the language behaviours we are predicting and how best we can predict them and also to what extent the S–P test (or similar knowledge-based test) does in fact capture the relevance of the individual's test responses to the behaviour areas under consideration: 'mere inspection of the test may fail to reveal the process actually used by subjects in taking the test' (Anastasi 1961:136).

My conclusion is not at all that we can abandon ESP testing, context-based testing or analysis of predicted language behaviour (indeed on one analysis the S–P test could be regarded as a very direct test indeed), rather that we should not be simplistic and naive about it. What is necessary is a thorough analysis at an appropriate (macro)linguistic level and an awareness of the significance in language behaviour both of abstraction and of underlying ability, capacity or competence, while accepting Anastasi's (1961:27) caveat that it is always *behaviour* that is tested ('no test can do more than measure behavior') but it is behaviour appropriately analysed ('a representative sample of the behavior domain to be measured').

My concern in commenting on this project has been with the interpretation of content validity and what is meant by a representative sample of the behaviour domain to be measured. Tests from this point of view are both samples *and* measures; tasks, however interesting, which are not both samples and measures are not tests. In my view this means that tests are more likely to be *indirect* than direct, that communicative tests are not strictly tests in the sense I have just described. However, they may still be tests in a different sense. 'Not all measurements are tests', says Tyler and 'the reverse is also true, not all tests are measurements. There are some personality tests, for example, that do not produce scores. A psychologist may use such a test to help him formulate a verbal description of a person. Measurement...need not be involved...' (Tyler 1971:23). Communicative tests then may have a place as ways of helping us formulate a verbal description of learners without enabling us to derive scores.

I have commented on classical views of content validity in this section, what Tyler calls asking the 'old validity' question: 'to what extent does this test measure what it purports to measure?' Tyler counsels us into asking what she does not call (but what presumably is) the *new* validity question: 'just what is it that this test does measure?' That no doubt is the way of language testing research in which tests are used as hypotheses. But for mainstream language testing we are still concerned with representative samples of behaviour domains to be measured, with the old validity question, even for communicative tests.

The second example of my Research Type 4 is only marginally concerned with language testing but it does apply language testing principles within applied linguistics to a type of evaluation, in this case to the evaluation of an influential book. My discussion here is based on the review I wrote (Davies 1981) of the book called *Communicative Syllabus Design* (Munby 1978).

I wrote the review because I thought the book was not about communication, not a syllabus and not about design − but that is neither here nor there. Munby's book has, in spite of the severe criticisms it has received (my own was only one among many), had considerable influence mainly because it provides a comprehensive and detailed account of the field of needs analysis. My view is that − the actual demerits of Munby's book apart − this is not the way to go about needs analysis. I prefer in any case *demands* analysis. What Munby is concerned with is a very static study of inter-role relationships and not with language at all. That is what is necessary in applied linguistics, that is what we attempted in our PLAB work, and that is why I provide here a summary of my view on the Munby book.

Communicative Syllabus Design (CSD)

This is an attempt to describe the general needs, or the language needs (it is never clear which), of foreign language learners. Certainly CSD is about needs and needs alone, which is a pity since the tension between needs and demands is one that is ripe for analysis. Needs are private, demands public, and it is arguable whether language teachers should be as much concerned with the former as with the latter. We are told that the book is an attempt to make up for the lack of a 'rigorous system for deriving syllabus specifications from adequate profiles of communication needs' (CSD:3). It does this 'by designing a dynamic processing model that starts with the learner and ends with his target communicative competence' (CSD:3). The model, we are told, must take account of discourse rules as well as grammatical ones (CSD:26−7). Chapter 2 is entitled 'Designing the Model: Parameters and Processes'. No theory is put forward, although this is the expectation set up by the word model. Theory, hypothesis, model − these all involve some scientific view which is falsifiable in some way; 'model' tends to be used when a weak claim is being made, but it is some kind of theoretical claim nonetheless; what Munby actually produces, however, is a linear set of important variables, and whether or not these are the only variables is never made clear.

Munby analyses his Communication Needs Processor (CNP) into eight variables 'that effect communication needs by organizing them as parameters in a dynamic relationship to each other' (CSD:32). Most of the parameters are necessary and helpful, although I suspect Munby underestimates the real difficulty of reaching the kind of specificity he strives for and also of being clear about such vague categories as setting and interaction. The apparatus provided (on pages 91−7) looks rigorous, but is entirely conjecture and must therefore be dismissed. Here Munby creates difficulties for himself since he insists that the CNP is concerned with communicative needs and not with language forms (CSD:40). Yet it is impossible to talk in measurement terms about target level and not get into language (Davies 1981).

The most unhappy of the CNP parameters is Communicative Key which is an attempt to specify the tone or manner or spirit in which a communicative event is carried out. To this end Munby has organized an Attitudinal Tone Index. The idea is that the Communicative Key allows the analyst to enter for every Communicative Event a specification of how that event is carried out. There are two problems here. The first is: how does Munby know? This Index comes entirely from his own intuition. The second is the stimulus− response problem. Munby provides stock responses but what happens when behaviour is not like this? What happens when the *authentic* breaks in? The Attitudinal Tone Index is not based on authentic data and is an attempt to provide pattern-like drills to indicate forms of modulation and mitigation.

The assumption the book seems to make is that if the complete model is applied then there will be certainty about the language output. This is not so, of course, because there is no way of being certain. Some language functions, like greetings, have a small number of possible language realizations. But most interesting functions do not, which is precisely why it is difficult to program computers for natural languages. As a set of specifications the Needs part is useful, but the sections on the language components are sheer metaphysics, unless given empirical tests. The book illustrates a problem of applied linguistics: how to remain applied and not slide into more prestigious theory. There is a strong temptation to build models in various areas of applied linguistics and then say take it or leave it. The models are not tested and indeed it is rare enough for some indication to be given as to how they might be tested. The danger (which Munby's diagrams, numbers, and formulae all increase) is that it will be taken as a model that works and not a model to speculate about. It will then be applied because it appears to provide solutions to enduring problems of language learning and teaching. The book would have made a more useful contribution to applied linguistics had it explicitly avoided any claims to an empirical basis.

Conclusion

The fundamental argument/debate in language testing over the last 25 years has been basically about the meaning/realization of language behaviour, how best to get at it. The issue is sometimes presented as if there were disagreement about language use. There is not. The disagreement is about the best way to capture control of that language use: this is the essence of the needs analysis, performance testing arguments. Knowledge, it is argued, is not equivalent to, nor indicative of behaviour. Behaviour is more complicated, more diverse. However, behaviour is very diffuse and when effectively sampled (for the sake of generality) less likely to be performance-like. Once again then a continuum can be set up from Language to Needs and the trick for testing is either to sample both (in which case the sampling of the Language must win out because it is more generalizable) or to try to bring them together in integrative tests, that is tasks which tap language on the job, work samples of the 1950s and 1960s now resurrected as performance tests. That is basically the Oller argument, though pragmatic tests are probably further off the central dimension of the continuum than they need be (see Table 21).

All tests require structure, a framework of some kind to preserve reliability. It looks as though the contribution of the communicative competence drive, of the move into communicative language teaching, will be to provide a little more validity in the shape of examples of language use. Tests will continue to use a combination of discrete point and integrative items and there will be a serious attempt to make the language provided in these items more realistic.

Testing procedures always need to be brought into step with teaching goals. That is correct from the point of view of pedagogy, but my argument in this book has been that there is a testing point of view to put alongside the

Table 21. Yet Another Continuum.

		+ Authentic	
Language	Pragmatic	Integrative	Needs
		Authentic −	

teaching one, and that in this case the testing view can act as a corrective to over-eager assumptions about teaching syllabuses. One important and relevant question to ask therefore is to what extent communicative language testing is feasible.

The typical extension of structuralist language frameworks (Lado 1961) could accommodate the testing of the communicative skills through, for example, context. Naturalism is a vulgar error: all education needs some measure of idealization and the search for authenticity in language teaching is chimerical (Davies 1984a). The linguist, the language teacher and the tester are all concerned with generalizing from a language sample to the whole of the language. Language is not divorced from communication and cannot be taught or tested separately. Testing (like teaching) the communicative skills is a way of making sure that there are tests of context as well as of grammar; testing (and teaching) the communicative skills is not doing something parallel to or different from testing (and teaching) the linguistic skills − what it does is to turn linguistics tests into language tests.

References

Alderson, J.C. (1979) 'The cloze procedure and proficiency in English as a foreign language'. *TESOL Quarterly*, 13:219–27.

Alderson, J.C., and Hughes, A. (eds) (1981) *Issues in Language Testing, ELT Documents 111*. London: The British Council.

Alderson, J.C., Krahnke, K.J. and Stansfield, C.W. (1987) *Reviews of English Language Proficiency Tests*. Washington, D.C.: TESOL.

Allen, J.P.B., and Davies, A. (eds) (1977) *Testing and Experimental Methods*. The Edinburgh Course in Applied Linguistics, Volume 4. Oxford: Oxford University Press.

Anastasi, A. (1961) *Psychological Testing*, 2nd ed. New York: Macmillan.

Anstey, E. (1966) *Psychological Tests*. London: Nelson.

Bachman, L.F. (1990) *Fundamental Considerations in Language Testing*. Oxford: Oxford University Press.

Bachman, L.F., and Palmer, A.S. (1982) 'The Construct Validation of the F.S.I. Oral Interview'. *Language Learning*, 31/1:67–86.

Beretta, A. (1962) Personal communication.

Beretta, A. (1986) 'Toward a methodology of ESL program evaluation'. *TESOL Quarterly* 20/1:144–55.

Beretta, A., and Davies, A. (1985) 'Evaluation of the Bangalore Project'. *ELT Journal*, 39/2:121–7.

Bernstein, B. (ed.) (1971) *Class Codes and Control*, Volume 1. London: Routledge, Kegan Paul.

Bormuth, J.R. (1970) *On the Theory of Achievement Test Items*. New York: University of Chicago Press.

Brindley, G. (1986) *The Assessment of Second Language Proficiency: Issues and Approaches*. Adelaide: N.C.R.C. Adult Migrant Education Program Australia Research Series.

Brown, S. (1981) *What do they know? A review of criterion-referenced assessment*. Edinburgh: HMSO.

Brumfit, C.J. (1984a) 'The Bangalore Procedural Syllabus'. *ELT Journal*, 38/4:233–41.

Brumfit, C.J. (1984b) *General English Syllabus Design, ELT Documents 118*. Oxford: Pergamon for British Council.

Butler, C. (1985) *Statistics in Linguistics* Oxford: Basil Blackwell.

Canale, M., and Swain, M. (1980) 'Theoretical Bases of Communicative Approaches to Second Language Teaching and Testing'. *Applied Linguistics*, 1/1:1–47.

Carroll, B.J. (1980) *Testing Communicative Performance*. Oxford: Pergamon.

Carroll, J.B. (1961) 'Fundamental Considerations in Testing for English-Language Proficiency of Foreign Students' in Allen, H.B., and Campbell, R.N. (eds) (1972) *Teaching English as a Second Language*. New York: McGraw-Hill, pp. 313–20.

Carroll, J.B., and Sapon, S.M. (1958) *Modern Language Aptitude Test*. New York: The Psychological Corporation.

Clark, J.L. (1987) *Curriculum Renewal in School Foreign Language Learning*. Oxford: Oxford University Press.

Corder, S.P. (1973) *Introducing Applied Linguistics*. Harmondsworth, Middlesex: Penguin.

Criper, C., and Davies, A. (1988) *ELTS Validation Project Report*, English Language Testing Service Research Report 1/1. Cambridge: British Council and U.C.L.E.S.

Cronbach, J.L. (1961) *Essentials of Psychological Testing*, 2nd ed. London: Harper and Row.

Crystal, D., Fletcher, P., and Garman, M. (1976) *The grammatical analysis of language disability*. London: Edward Arnold.

Davies, A. (1971) 'Language Aptitude in the First Year of the UK Secondary School' in *RELC Journal*, 2/1:4–19.

Davies, A. (1975) 'Two tests of speeded reading' in Jones and Spolsky, pp. 119–27.

Davies, A. (1977) 'The Construction of Language Tests', Chapter 3 in Allen, J.P.B., and Davies, A. (eds) *Testing and Experimental Methods*, Vol. 4 of *Edinburgh Course in Applied Linguistics*. Oxford: Oxford University Press, pp. 38–104.

Davies, A. (1978) 'Language Testing', Parts 1 & 2 in *Language Teaching and Linguistics Abstracts* Cambridge University Press: 11/3:145–59, 11/4:215–31; reprinted in Kinsella, V. (ed.) (1982) *Surveys*. Cambridge: Cambridge University Press.

Davies, A. (1981) Review of Munby, J. (1978) *Communicative Syllabus Design*. Cambridge: Cambridge University Press, in *TESOL Quarterly*, 332–6.

Davies, A. (1983a) *English Language Testing in the University of Edinburgh, report on the English Language Battery (ELBA) with an analysis of results 1973–79*. University of Edinburgh: unpublished.

Davies, A. (1983b) *Report on a Visit to South India, February 1983: Evaluation and the Bangalore/Madras Communicational Language Teaching Project*. London, British Council: unpublished.

Davies, A. (1984a) 'Simple, simplified and simplification: what is authentic?' in Alderson, J.C., and Urquhart, A.H. (eds) *Reading in a Foreign Language*. London: Longman, pp. 181–98.

Davies, A. (1984b) 'Validating Three Tests of English Language Proficiency'. *Language Testing*, 1/1:50–69.

Davies, A. (1985) 'Follow my leader: is that what language tests do?' in Lee, V.P. *et al.* pp. 3–13.

Davies, A. (1986) 'Indirect ESP testing: Old innovations' in Portal, M. pp. 55–67.

Davies, A. (1987) 'When professional advice and political constraints conflict: the case of Nepal', *Focus on English*, Madras: British Council.

Davies, A. (1988a) 'Operationalising Uncertainty in Language Testing, an Argument in Favour of Content Validity'. *Language Testing*, 5/1:32–48.

Davies, A. (1988b) *Report on the Evaluation of the Communicative Teaching of English Project*. London, British Council: unpublished.

Davies, A. (1989) 'Testing reading speed through text retrieval' in Candlin C.N. and T.F. McNamara (eds) *Language, Learning and Community*, New South Wales, N.C.E.L.: 115–24.

Davies, A. (ed.) (1968) *Language Testing Symposium*. Oxford: Oxford University Press.

Davies, A., Glendinning, E., and Maclean, A. (1984) *Survey of English Language Teaching in Nepal*. Report by British Council/ODA Survey team to HMGN Ministry of Education and Culture, Kathmandu: unpublished.

Della Piana, G.M., and Endo, G.T. (1973) 'Reading Research' in Travers, R.M.W. (ed.) *Second Handbook of Research on Teaching*. Chicago: Rand McNally for A.E.R.A., pp. 883–925.

ELTDU (n.d.) *English Language Teaching Development Unit — O.U.P. Stages of Attainment Scale*, Stage G Test. Colchester: ELTDU.

Eysenck, H.J. (1953) *Uses and Abuses of Psychology*. Harmondsworth, Middlesex: Penguin.

Gibson, E.J., and Levin, H. (1976) *The Psychology of Reading*. Cambridge, Mass.: M.I.T. Press.

Glaser, G.R. (1963) 'Instructional technology and the measurement of learning outcomes'. *American Psychologist*, 18:519–21.

Greenwood, J. (1985) 'Bangalore revisited: a reluctant complaint'. *ELT Journal*, 39/4:268–73.

Grieve, D.W. (1964) *English Language Examining*. Ibadan: African Universities Press for the West African Examinations Council.

Harris, D.P. (1969) *Testing English as a Second Language*. New York: McGraw-Hill.

Hatch, E., and Farhady, H. (1982) *Research Design and Statistics for Applied Linguistics*. Rowley, Mass.: Newbury House.

Heaton, J.B. (1975) *Writing English Language Tests*. London: Longman. (2nd ed. 1988)

Henning, G. (1987) *A Guide to Language Testing*. Cambridge, Mass.: Newbury House.

Howatt, A.P.R., and Davies, A. (1979) *ELBA Testing 1973–77: Interim Report on analysis of Results*. Edinburgh University Department of Linguistics, unpublished.

Hughes, A. (1989) *Testing for Language Teachers*. Cambridge: Cambridge University Press.

Hughes, A., and Porter, D. (eds) (1983) *Current Developments in Language Testing*. New York: Academic Press.

Ingram, E. (1973) 'English Standards of Foreign Students'. *Edinburgh University Bulletin*, May.

Jones, R., and Spolsky, B. (eds) (1975) *Testing Language Proficiency*. Washington: Center for Applied Linguistics.

Kennedy, C. (ed.) (1983) *Language Planning and Language Education*. London: G. Allen and Unwin.

Klein-Braley, C., and Raatz, U. (1984) 'A Survey of Research on the C-Test'. *Language Testing* 1/2:134–46.

Krashen, S.D. (1982) *Principles and Practice in Second Language Acquisition*. Oxford: Pergamon.

Lado, R. (1961) *Language Tests: the Construction and Use of Foreign Language Tests*. London: Longman.

Lee, Y.P., Fok, A.C.C., Lord, R., and Low, G. (eds) (1985) *New Directions in Language Testing*. Oxford: Pergamon.

Long, M.H. (1984) 'Process and Product in ESL Program Evaluation'. *TESOL Quarterly*, 18/3:409–25.

Madsen, H. (1983) *Techniques in Testing*. Oxford: Oxford University Press.

Manning, W.H. (1987) *Development of Cloze-elide Tests of English as a Second Language*, TOEFL Research Report 23. (April). Princeton, N.J.: Educational Testing Service.

Masters, G.N. (1982) 'A Rasch Model for partial credit scoring'. *Psychometrika*, 47:149–74.

Morrow, K.E. (1977) *Techniques of Evaluation for a Notional Syllabus.* London: Royal Society of Arts.

Morrow, K.E. (1979) 'Communicative language testing: revolution or evolution?' in Brumfit, C.J., and Johnson, K. (eds) *The Communicative Approach to Language Teaching.* London: Oxford University Press, pp. 143–57.

Munby, J. (1978) *Communicative Syllabus Design.* Cambridge: Cambridge University Press.

Oller, J.W. (1976) 'A program for language testing research' in Brown, H.D. (ed.) *Papers in second language acquisition. Language Learning,* pp. 141–66.

Oller, J.W. (1979) *Language Tests at School.* London: Longman.

Oller, J.W. (ed.) (1983) *Issues in Language Testing Research.* Rowley, Mass.: Newbury House.

Pienemann, M., and Johnson, M. (1984) 'Towards an explanatory model of language acquisition'. Paper presented at the 9th ALAA Congress, Alice Springs, 29 Aug.–2 Sept. 1984: unpublished.

Pimsleur, P. (1966) *Language Aptitude Battery.* New York: Harcourt, Brace and World.

Portal, M. (ed.) (1986) *Innovations in Language Testing.* London: NFER/Nelson.

Prabhu, N.S. (1987) *Second Language Pedagogy.* Oxford: Oxford University Press.

Prator, C. (1978) 'The British Heresy in TESL' in Fishman, J.A., Ferguson, C.A., and Das Gupta, J. (eds) *Language Problems of Developing Nations.* New York: Wiley and Sons.

Quinn, T.J., and McNamara, T.F. (1988) *Issues in Second Language Learning: General and Particular.* Brisbane: Deakin University.

Ross, J.R. (1979) 'Where's English?' in Fillmore, C.J., Kemper, D., and Wang, W.S.-Y. (eds) *Individual Differences in Language Ability and Language Behavior.* New York: Academic Press, pp. 127–163

Royal Society of Arts (1980) *Examinations in the Communicative Use of English as a Foreign Language.* London: Royal Society of Arts.

Sapir, E. (1921) *Language: an introduction to the Study of Speech.* New York: Harcourt, Brace and World.

Savignon, S. (1986) 'Evaluation of Communicative Competence in relation to the TOEFL Program' in Stansfield, C.W. (ed.), pp. 17–30.

Skehan, P. (1988) 'Language Testing', Parts 1 & 2. *Language Teaching Abstracts,* Cambridge: Cambridge University Press.

Skehan, P. (1989) *Individual Differences in Second and Foreign Language Learning.* London: Edward Arnold.

Smith, D.J. (1980) *Overseas Doctors in the N.H.S.* London: Heinemann.

Smith, P.D., Jr (1970) *A Comparison of the Cognitive and Audiolingual Approaches to Foreign Language Instruction: the Pennsylvania Foreign Language Project.* Philadelphia, Penn.: Center for Curriculum Development.

Spolsky, B. (1977) 'Language testing: Art or Science?' in Nickel, G. (ed.) *Proceedings of the Fourth International Congress of Applied Linguistics,* Volume 3. Stuttgart: Hochschulverlag.

Spolsky, B. (1989) *Conditions for Second Language Learning.* Oxford: Oxford University Press.

Stansfield, C.W. (ed.) (1986) *Toward Communicative Competence Testing: Proceedings of the Second TOEFL Invitational Conference,* TOEFL Research Report 21. Princeton, N.J.: Educational Testing Service.

Sutcliffe, D. (1982) *British Black English.* Oxford: Basil Blackwell.

Tinker, M.A. (1965) *Bases for Effective Reading*. Minneapolis: University of Minnesota Press.

Tyler, L.E. (1971) *Tests and Measurements*, 2nd ed. Englewood Cliffs, N.J.: Prentice-Hall.

Valette, R.M. (1967) *Modern Language Testing: a Handbook*, 1st ed. New York: Harcourt, Brace and World.

Valette, R.M. (1977) *Modern Language Testing*, 2nd ed. New York: Harcourt Brace Jovanovich.

Valette, R.M., and Disick, R.S. (1972) *Modern Language Performance: Objectives and individualization*. New York: Harcourt Brace Jovanovich.

van Ek, J.A. (1980) *The Threshold Level*. Strasbourg: Council of Europe and Oxford: Pergamon.

Weir, C.J. (1988) *Communicative Language Testing, with special reference to English as a Foreign Language*. Exeter University. Exeter Linguistic Series No. 11.

Wright, P. (1968) 'Reading to Learn'. *Chemistry in Britain* 4.

Journals:
Language Testing (1984–), twice a year. London: Edward Arnold.
Language Testing Update. University of Lancaster.

Index of Subjects

Index of Names